1991

# THE SOUTH'S ROLE IN THE CREATION OF THE BILL OF RIGHTS

# The South's Role in the Creation of the Bill of Rights

*Essays by*
JACK P. GREENE
DAVID THOMAS KONIG
EDWARD C. PAPENFUSE, JR.
WALTER F. PRATT, JR.
JAMES W. ELY, JR.
PETER CHARLES HOFFER

*Edited by*
ROBERT J. HAWS

UNIVERSITY PRESS OF MISSISSIPPI
Jackson and London

The paper in this book meets the guidelines for permanence and
durability of the Committee on Production Guidelines for Book
Longevity of the Council on Library Resources.


**Library of Congress Cataloging-in-Publication Data**

The South and the creation of the Bill of Rights : essays by Jack P.
    Greene . . . [et al.] / edited by Robert J. Haws.
        p.   cm.
    Includes bibliographical references and index.
    ISBN 0-87805-494-4
    1. Slavery—Law and Legislation—Southern States—History.
2. Afro-Americans—Legal status, laws, etc.—Southern States-
-History.   3. Civil rights—Southern States—History.   I. Haws,
Robert J.   II. Greene, Jack P.
KF4545.S5S68   1991
342.75′085—dc20                                                    90-21707
[347.50285]                                                        CIP


British Library Cataloguing-in-Publication data available

# Contents

Introduction        3

The Constitution of 1787 and the Question of Southern
    Distinctiveness        9
JACK P. GREENE

Natural Rights, Bills of Rights, and the People's Rights
    in Virginia Constitutional Discourse, 1787–1791        33
DAVID THOMAS KONIG

The "Amending Fathers" and the Constitution:
    Changing Perceptions of Home Rule and Who Should Rule
    at Home        51
EDWARD C. PAPENFUSE, JR.

Oral and Written Cultures: North Carolina
    and the Constitution, 1787–1791        77
WALTER F. PRATT, JR.

"The Good Old Cause": The Ratification of the Constitution
    and Bill of Rights in South Carolina        101
JAMES W. ELY, JR.

Constitutional Silences: Georgia, the Constitution, and the Bill
    of Rights—A Historical Test of Originalism        125
PETER CHARLES HOFFER

Notes        147

Contributors        179

Index        181

# THE SOUTH'S ROLE IN THE CREATION OF THE BILL OF RIGHTS

# Introduction: The South and the Origins of United States Constitutionalism, 1787–1791

The idea of region has animated a large share of American historical scholarship for the last century. Numerous scholars have argued that an understanding of divergent regional interests is essential to an understanding of national developments in the United States. For purposes of historical analysis, it is also clear that any definition of regional identity must encompass two principal themes. First of all, those living outside a region must perceive that such a region exists. Second, a sense common interest must exist among the inhabitants of a region to the extent that they perceive themselves to be part of a distinctive regional culture. The United States is a nation of regions and the basis and timing for the emergence of American regions varies greatly throughout the American history. New England existed as a region in the seventeenth century while the Pacific Northwest is a twentieth century phenomenon.

One of the more intriguing issues of southern history is to determine the origins and basis of a southern regional identity. It has become increasingly clear that the beginnings of a distinctive southern regionalism appear in the era of the American Revolution. The idea of a southern interest, however nebulous in its infancy, became a factor at the Constitutional Convention in the summer of 1787 and in the struggle for ratification of the Constitution and the Bill of Rights. Southern delegates were generally more committed than delegates from other parts of the country to a

3

governmental structure which would neither challenge the rights of the states in any significant way nor threaten the deeply ingrained tradition of local autonomy which the widely dispersed people of the region cherished. The economic and social importance of the institution of slavery in the southern seaboard states partially explains this growing sense of regional identity, but any definition southern regionalism goes well-beyond a "knee-jerk" defense of slavery.

The tradition of local autonomy which southern delegates so determinedly defended at Philadelphia has its origins in the colonial period of American history. The American Revolution was, after all, a struggle between central and local authority within the British Empire. The concern for preservation of local autonomy was reflected in the structure of government under the Articles of Confederation and persisted in the Constitutional Convention. The delicate balance between state and national authority established at Philadelphia was intended to protect regional and local interests. The reasons for this persistent localism are obvious. Many delegates in Philadelphia, particularly those from the southern seaboard states, believed that perservation of local autonomy was the surest way to protect liberty.

The federal system established by the Constitution created the political/constitutional arena which nurtured regionalism. The observation made by the distinguished southern historian Charles Sackett Sydnor that the twin sources of authority in southern history were the Bible and the Constitution highlights two of the more important elements which have served to establish a distinctive regional identity in the America South.[1] Religious fundamentalism as a factor in defining the South emerged only in the early nineteenth-century. It is in the struggles over the Constitution, however, where historians have found the first substantial evidence of an emerging regional identity. From the Constitution, southerners fashioned a "cultural constitutionalism" intended to preserve a tradition of localism which assured the preservation of many of the most distinctive features of the region, including, but not exclusively, protection for slavery. While that tradition of local autonomy has been significantly eroded during the last half century, it still helps define the contemporary South.

The essays which follow reveal how delegates from the five states from the Chesapeake to Spanish Florida sought to draft a new frame of government which would at once establish a viable union of states and protect the essential elements of an emerging sense of regional identity. The struggle to assure local autonomy continued into the ratification conventions of each state. It was during this struggle in United States history that constitutionalism and cultural identity joined. As Kermit Hall and James W. Ely, Jr. have argued, this cultural constitutionalism comprised features common to most of the United States at the time, but the South's peculiar response to "racism, states' rights and individual liberty . . . [help illuminate] the place of the South in the American constitutional tradition."[2]

It became common by the mid-eighteenth century for talented observers of colonial America to describe cultural differences found in the various regions of British North America. Jack Greene describes with great dexterity the subtleties of these distinctions as perceived by late-eighteenth century Americans and visitors to America. The most obvious and most important of these features in the early years of the republic was, of course, slavery. In these years, however, no monolithic regional response to slavery was apparent. As Greene emphasizes, delegates from the Chesapeake states of Maryland and Virginia took a decidedly less strident approach to issues related to slavery at the Constitutional Convention than did their counterparts from the southern seaboard states of South Carolina and Georgia. Greene notes, however, that "during the struggle over the Constitution," American political leaders, "were coming to define national political life in terms of a broad north-south division. . . ."[3] In constitutional terms, it was the interplay of the defensive attitude toward slavery, the desire to protect the rights of the states in the new federal union and the concern for the preservation of individual liberties that began the process of setting the southern states apart from the rest of the union.

The two Chesapeake states provide interesting and significantly different problems associated with the Constitution. David Thomas Konig describes the contradictions and uncertainties which existed among the members of the Virginia delegation in Philadelphia and which continued into the state's ratification convention. He shows how the uncertainties that Virginians had about the capacity of the new Constitution to circumscribe governmental power go well beyond a desire to protect slavery. A dual irony existed among the Virginia political leadership. Those most opposed to the consolidation of national power supported the adoption of a Bill of Rights thereby implicitly accepting the notion of an expansive governmental power. Those who supported the strengthening of the national government argued that the new government was one of limited, delegated powers and constituted no real threat to either the states or to local autonomy. Virginians sought a government which would secure a viable union and pose no threat to such matters of local concern as slavery or criminal jury trials.

An even more chaotic localism plagued the ratification process in Maryland. As Edward C. Papenfuse, Jr., argues, Maryland politicians seemed more interested in protecting bastions of local political power than taking part in any sophisticated discussion of individual rights or the protection of slavery. The ratification of the Constitution presented an "unprecedented challenge to the long-standing, peaceful hegemony of the governing elite . . ."[4] According to Papenfuse, this incipient democracy fundamentally transformed the course of Maryland politics. Such a change would have been impossible without the preservation of local political autonomy under the Constitution.

The southern seaboard states of South Carolina and Georgia each present different problems in explaining the acceptance of the Constitution. South Carolina sent one of the most influential delegations to Philadelphia, Georgia one of the least influential.

South Carolina delegates took the lead in protecting slavery under the new Constitution, going as far as threatening to bolt the convention during the debate over the importation of slaves. Abraham Baldwin of Georgia, in one of his few comments at the Convention, insisted that slavery was a local matter best left to state jurisdiction. As James W. Ely, Jr. and Peter Hoffer point out in their essays, both states were wedded to slavery. Ely finds some of the same impulses that Papenfuse found in Maryland. Both states were dominated by a propertied elite which wanted to use the new Constitution to preserve its power base. The South Carolinians were more successful than their counterparts in Maryland.

The record of Georgia's ratification of the Constitution is quite sparse and the state failed to ratify the Bill of Rights. Nevertheless, Peter Hoffer imaginatively discusses the constitutionalism of the states's political leaders by examining the state constitutional convention and the state's response to *Chisholm v. Georgia*. As Hoffer points out, the state constitution drew heavily from the new federal Constitution as the framers sought to overcome the excessive populism of the first state constitution and *Chisholm* posed "the first genuine challenge to the supremacy clause of the Constitution, the authority of the Supreme Court, and the legislative power of Congress."[5] These examples reveal the determination of Georgia's political leaders to preserve their local autonomy.

North Carolina was the only state not to ratify the Constitution the first time around. Walter F. Pratt, Jr. approaches this problem in a non-traditional manner. He finds the distinctions between written and oral traditions help understand the divisions over the Constitution. Further, such distinctions also reveal subtle class distinctions in North Carolina. As the state which served the most minimal role in the writing and ratification of the Constitution and the adoption of the Bill of Rights, North Carolina's political leaders, like those in Maryland were most concerned about the preservation of local autonomy. Only when a Bill of Rights was adopted by Congress did North Carolina reconsider and ratify the Constitution.

It is clear from the history of the writing and ratification of the Constitution and Bill of Rights that no monolithic South existed in 1791. Virginia's political leaders, for example, did not find themselves bound by a constricted sense of regional identity. Only in the late 1820s and early 1830s, did the leadership of the Old Dominion begin to reveal an identity more regional than national. Nevertheless, the seeds of that regional identity which made the South distinctive are found first in the years between 1787 and 1791. In helping shape the structure of the new Republic, southern slaveholders shaped it in their own image. In their efforts to preserve that structure, historians have found the origins of a southern regional interest. These essays provide a reasonably complete discussion of writing and ratification of the Constitution in the South and the manner in which that process gradually became an important part of an emerging regional identity. As such, the process constitutes a necessary early step in the emergence of the South as a distinctive regional culture in the United States.

Earlier versions of the essays which comprise this volume were presented at the thirteenth Porter L. Fortune, Jr., Symposium on Southern History at the University of Mississippi in October 1987. The Symposium received the generous support of the Mississippi Humanities Council and on behalf of the University, I would like to extend a special thanks to Cora Norman, the council's executive director, and Barbara Carpenter, the council's associate director for their continued support. This annual symposium has also benefitted from the continued support of Chancellor R. Gerald Turner and Dean H. Dale Abadie. As usual, the entire faculty of the department of history and the staff of the Center for the Study of Southern Culture did "yeoman duty" in order to make the symposium a success.

R.J.H.

# The Constitution of 1787 and the Question of Southern Distinctiveness

JACK P. GREENE

## I

Historians of the southern colonies and states during the seventeenth and eighteenth centuries can only welcome the devotion of several annual meetings of a major symposium on southern history to the origins of the South in the colonial and early national periods. Historians of the South, it seems to an outsider such as myself, have concentrated largely upon only a few major themes: the character and institutions of the Old South at the pinnacle—or the nadir—of its development between 1830 and 1860; the South's gallant but unsuccessful defense of its way of life during the Civil War and, for the South, the humiliating aftermath of that war; the intermittent and difficult efforts thereafter to build a New South in the image of the North; and the continuing burden of the region's past upon its present.

As a result of their efforts, the defining characteristics of the Old South, the central features that, despite significant regional variations, bound the southern states together as a single socio-cultural unit and formed the basis for the articulation of a distinctive and region-wide sectional identity, are well known. These include plantation agriculture, a racially prescribed system among an agricultural elite, an unsystematic pattern of land occupation, weak commercial infrastructures, high levels of economic growth combined with low levels of economic development, and dominance of political institutions by a family-conscious and increasingly exclusive elite. These highly visible social features were combined with a distinctive mentality that was anti-capitalistic, if not "feudal"; deeply committed to an agrarian way of life; uninterested, if not actually hostile, to economic and technological innovation; self-consciously traditional and backward-looking in its cultivation of civility and other European upper-class values and in its suspicion of change; defensive about its continuing commitment to slavery in a era when that institution was being abandoned by most of the rest of the civilized world; acutely aware of its minority position within the American political union; and vigorously assertive of states rights against the authority of the national government.

The relative disinterest of students of the Old South in the history of the region before the 1820s and 1830s has contributed to considerable confusion over several important questions. Of particular importance are the highly general questions of whether this cluster of characteristics that seems for the mid-nineteenth century to define the South as a coherent and distinctive segment of American culture had always been present among the several societies that subsequently come to comprise the South and, if not, when and why those characteristics appeared.

In specific relation to the subject of this symposium, these general questions can be refined into several more precise ones: To what extent was there an entity we can call the South, a First South, the antecedent of the Old South, at the time of the fabrication of the Federal Constitution in 1787–88? To what extent was that entity already a distinctive—even a deviant—component of the emerging American cultural order? To what extent did leaders of the "southern" states manifest an awareness of the existence either of such an entity or of the common features that composed it? To what extent did such an awareness shape their actions in 1787–88? Some preliminary answers to these questions, all of which are implicit in the title of this symposium, are necessary before the role of the southern states in the constitutional era can be fully appreciated.

## II

That there was a broad socio-cultural fault line separating the southern colonies from the northern colonies and that there were significant behavioral and characterological differences between inhabitants of the two regions was already widely asserted by contemporaries during the era of the American Revolution. Thomas Jefferson's brief commentary on these differences to the Marquis de Chastellux in 1785 is well known. North of Pennsylvania, Jefferson observed, people were "cool, sober, laborious, independent, jealous of their own liberties, and just to those of others, interested, chicaning, and superstitious and hypocritical in their religion." From Maryland south, by contrast, people were "fiery, voluptuary, indolent, unsteady, zealous for their own liberties, but trampling on those of others, generous, candid, and without attachments or pretentions to any religion but that of the heart."[1]

But others anticipated Jefferson's remarks with even fuller analyses of this phenomenon. One of the most impressive of these was by the London Quaker philanthropist, Dr. John Fothergill, who summed up a century and a half of impressions among informed London opinion in his *Considerations Relative to the North American Colonies*, a pamphlet pleading for the repeal of the Stamp Act published in London in 1765. Cautioning his readers not to identify "the Inhabitants of *North America*" with those of the "*West-India* Islands," he noted that the "*British* Inhabitants of *North America*" were "of two Sorts; those who live[d] in the northern Part of the Continent, and those who inhabit[ed] the Southern. *Nova Scotia, New England* and its Dependencies, *New York*, the *Jerseys* and *Pensilvania*," he wrote, "belong[ed] to the former Division: *Maryland* may be divided between both; *Virginia*, the *Carolinas* and *Georgia*, are the other Part."

What accounted for these two broad behavioral groupings, according to Fothergill, were contrasting physical environments and configurations of socio-economic life. "The Inhabitants of the northern Part," Fothergill wrote, "live like our lower *English* Farmers; they plough, sow, reap, and vend different Kinds of Grain, as the Land they occupy and the Climate permits; Maize, Wheat, Barley, Oats, Pease, and the like rural Produce. They raise Cattle, Hogs, and other Domestick Animals for Use and Sale; also Hemp, Flax, [and] Naval Stores. . . . Their Summers are hot, their Winters severe, and their Lives are passed with the like Labour and Toil . . . as the little Farmers in *England*." A few people, also as in England, went into trade and, "aided by Capacity and Industry," thereby raised themselves "above the Level." Even though they could obtain land cheaply, marry young, and, in most cases, count on at least a modest inheritance, however, most people had to be satisfied with acquiring little more than was "sufficient to maintain their Families just above Want." If they could "afford to have an *English* Utensil, or *English* Cloathing," they considered themselves "rich."

By contrast, the inhabitants of the southern North American colonies "approach[ed much] nearer to the *West Indians*." Their lands were "capable of producing Riches of another Nature; Tobacco," that "pleasing Intoxication of many Nations," was produced in "*Maryland* and *Virginia*, chiefly by the Labour of Negroes." Rice was "the Product of the *Carolinas*, a happy Succedaneum for Bread; [and] the proper, the most suitable Support of hot Countries," which was "likewise . . . raised, cultivated, [and] dress'd by the Labour of Negroes." "Properly cultivated," a few acres of the liberal soils of these southern North American colonies, like those in the West Indies, thus yielded crops that were far more saleable and considerably superior in value to those produced on much larger plots in the north, and higher profits permitted the owners to purchase the black slaves whose heavy toils both exempted their owners from the obligation of "labour[ing] for themselves" and enabled them to become comparatively rich. "Surrounded in their

Infancy with a numerous Retinue of" slaves, moreover, whites in this area became "habituated by Precept and Example, to Sensuality, Selfishness, and Despotism" and addicted to "Splendor, Dress, Shew, Equipage, [and] every thing that can create an Opinion of their Importance."

Whereas "the Northern People of *America*" thus had to "trust to their own Industry," "Southern Inhabitants" were "rich in Proportion to the Number of Slaves they possess[ed]." Whereas the northern colonies were populated mostly by "low and middling People" and had few or none who were "great or rich," the southern colonies had "few middling People, a very few" of whom were "considerable, [with all] the rest . . . below the middle Class in general." Whereas northerners were industrious, "contented with a little, [and excellent] Examples of Diligence and Frugality, the best Riches of a State," southerners were "too often the Reverse," enervated, given to "Idleness and Extravagance," unable to "be contented with Mediocrity," and lustful "to contrive every Means of Gratification."[2]

Fothergill's contention that southern North Americans and the southern colonies had more in common with West Indians and the West Indian colonies than with northern North Americans and the northern colonies presents an image of the southern continental colonies and their free inhabitants that is reasonably compatible with modern historical portraits of the Old South and its inhabitants. In all probability, however, the distinctions made by Fothergill were much more clearly understood in London than in any of the colonies. Despite a growing volume of contacts among the colonies through the middle decades of the eighteenth century, each colony still represented a discrete and largely self-contained political environment that was much more closely connected to London, and probably also even more familiar to informed observers in the metropolis, than it was to any of its immediate neighbors in America.

But the American Revolution abruptly changed this situation. Once united resistance had begun in the mid-1770s, close associations in the Continental Congresses and in the army brought large numbers of people from all the colonies together in the common cause of resisting British policy and seeking to establish American independence. To an important degree, this process helped to impress many people with a strong sense of a commonality among the colonies, commonalities not just of interest in seeking these common goals but also in culture and orientation. Thus could Benjamin Rush credibly insist in congressional debate during the summer of 1776 that, whatever the continuing variety among the new American states, their interests, "Trade, Language, Customs, and Manners," were by no means "more divided than they are among . . . people in Britain."[3] But more intense and sustained contact also produced a heightened awareness of regional diversities in interest, cultural configurations, and character. Indeed, that contact no doubt helped in many instances to confirm long-building stereotypes and to intensify the suspicions and the distrust implicit in those stereotypes.

"The Characters of Gentlemen in the four New England Colonies," John Adams wrote to Joseph Hawley in November 1775, "differ from those in the others . . . as much as [in] several distinct Nations almost. Gentlemen, Men of Sense, or any Kind of Education in the other Colonies are much fewer in Proportion than in N[ew] England," Adams thought, expressing his customary sectional pride: "Gentlemen, in the other Colonies have large Plantations of slaves, and the common People among them are very ignorant and very poor. These Gentlemen are accustomed, habituated to higher Notions of themselves and the distinction between them and the common People, than We are." Ever the realist, Adams understood that it would be difficult to fabricate an American union and an American identity out of such discordant materials, and he stressed the improbability of ever bringing about any fundamental change in "the Character of a Colony, and that Temper and those Sentiments which its Inhabitants imbibed with their Mother[']s Milk, and which have grown with their Growth and strengthened with their Strength."[4]

More cautious delegates especially continued to doubt that any effective or lasting union among such heterogeneous components could ever turn out well. "Their different Forms of Government— Productions of Soil—and Views of Commerce, their different Religions—Tempers and private Interest—their Prejudices against, and Jealousies of, each other—all have, and ever will, from the Nature and Reason of things, conspire to create such a Diversity of Interests, Inclinations, and Decisions, that they never can [long] unite together even for their own Protection," predicted Joseph Galloway: "In this Situation Controversies founded in Interest, Religion or Ambition, will soon embrue their Hands in the blood of each other."[5] Not just timid and future loyalists like Galloway but also ardent proponents of continental union like John Adams worried about the long-range prospects of a union of such apparently disparate parts. "I dread the Consequences of this Disimilitude of Character" among the colonies, Adams wrote, "and without the Utmost Caution . . . and the most prudent Condescention . . . , they will certainly be fatal."[6]

Whether the American Union might split along sectional lines and what those sections might be were, however, questions about which there was a great variety of opinion. When John Dickinson worried in July 1776 about the eventual dissolution of the American union, he drew the line not between the slave-powered staple economies of the south and the mixed agricultural and commercial economies of the north but between New England and the rest of the states.[7] West and south of the New York-New England border, in fact, distrust of New England was chronic and widespread throughout the revolutionary era and beyond. Indeed, very few people in the 1770s and 1780s seem to have thought in terms of a consolidated northern interest, and many carefully distinguished among the "Eastern" or four New England states, and the "Middle" states from New York south to and sometimes including Maryland and even Virginia. Alexander Hamilton expressed this increasingly conventional point of view in *Federalist* #13 when he predicted that any break up of the union would be followed by the

establishment of three confederacies, one composed of the four
northern or New England states, a second of the four middle
states, and a third of the five southern states.[8]

Recent scholarship on the socio-economic and cultural development of Britain's North American colonies during the early modern era has tended to confirm the accuracy and utility of this more
complex and subtle sectional analysis. During the last two decades, scholars have analyzed the socio-economic landscape of
colonial British America more deeply and more extensively than
ever before, and they have increasingly come to conceptualize that
landscape in terms of several clearly distinguishable regions. On
the basis of what has been essentially a functional analysis of
emerging socio-economic configurations and cultural orientations
in colonial British America, historians have charted the development of not three but five broad culture areas by the last half of
the eighteenth century, two northern, two southern, and one
western.

Identical with those defined by the Revolutionary generation
themselves, the two northern are New England, composed of the
four New England colonies, Nova Scotia, and after 1775, Vermont,
and the Middle colonies, including New York, New Jersey, Pennsylvania, and Delaware. The two southern regions are the
Chesapeake or Upper South, consisting of Virginia, Maryland,
and the northern half of North Carolina, and the Lower South,
composed of South Carolina, the southern half of North Carolina,
Georgia, and after 1763, East and West Florida. The western
region is the New West, the broad arc of inland settlements
stretching from western Pennsylvania south into Georgia and
then, after 1770, west into Kentucky and Tennessee.

To be sure, the Chesapeake and the Lower South shared many
important attributes. These included a strong commitment to
plantation agriculture and black slavery, an economy oriented
heavily towards agricultural and extractive exports, relatively high
levels of wealth and property consolidation among the free population, a marked interest in economic and technological innovation,

high levels of white immigration, and, at least in the older colonies of Virginia, Maryland, and South Carolina, stable political leadership. But there were also significant differences between these two regions. The Chesapeake had a much larger population with a substantially greater proportion of whites; lower per capita wealth among whites; a considerably more diverse agricultural and manufacturing economy; a large slave population whose vigorous natural growth was by the 1760s sufficient to make it unnecessary to import many new slaves; and a slave system in which most slaves lived under the direct management of white families, many on smaller units of production, and thus enjoyed relatively little autonomy and were strongly subjected to the assimilative pressures of white paternalism.

The Lower South, by contrast, had a smaller population with a much higher ratio of blacks to whites; a less diversified economy; a proportionately considerably greater commitment to plantation agriculture and a continuing high demand for slave imports; and a slave system in which blacks, consisting of a much higher percentage of native Africans, concentrated on larger units, and mostly working by the task system with a minimum of white supervision, had considerably more autonomy in their daily lives and were able to preserve far more of their African heritage. To the west of both these areas and including a large proportion of North Carolina, the New West, with a smaller concentration of slaves and only a limited involvement with plantation agriculture, still more resembled the mixed farming areas of the middle colonies and the fringe areas of the Chesapeake than it did the cultural core of either the Upper or the Lower South.[9]

Perhaps because of this considerable diversity among the southern states as well as because, as H. James Henderson's studies of divisions in the Confederation Congress reveal, patterns of voting in the national arena, very often cut across sectional lines,[10] not many people during these years seem in fact to have thought in terms of a distinctive "southern" interest that might have provided the basis for a political alliance among these several "southern" regions. When, in 1778, he expressed alarm at the possibility that, according to the Articles of Confederation, the nine other states might drive through Congress "the most important transactions . . . contrary to the united opposition of Virginia, the two Carolinas and Georgia," William Henry Drayton of South Carolina was one of the few who seems to have had an acute appreciation of the possibility that "the nature of the climate, soil and produce of the several states" would "naturally and unavoidably" give rise to a distinctive "northern and southern interest in many particulars."[11]

In the Philadelphia Convention itself and in the ratifying conventions that followed, delegates used a wide range of categories to describe the divergent interests within the United States, and these categories were almost invariably framed in terms of polar opposites. They talked in terms of large states vs. small states, commercial states vs. non-commercial (sometimes referred to as landed or agricultural) states,[12] carrying states vs. non-carrying (sometimes called productive) states,[13] and distant vs. central states.[14] John Rutledge of South Carolina even anticipated a future division between Atlantic states and western states.[15] Within the Convention, however, the perception that the most important division among the states revolved around the distinction between the northern states and the southern states and that that division had been and would continue to be fundamental to national political life quickly acquired the status of a self-evident truth.

As was the case with so many other aspects of the Convention debates, James Madison was responsible for initially articulating this perception. Trying to allay the fears of delegates from the small states that a representational system based on population might deprive the small states of their identity as states and leave them at the mercy of the large states, Madison on June 30 observed, in an oft-cited remark, "that the States were divided into different interests not by their differences of size, but by other circumstances; the most material of which resulted partly from climate, but principally from the effects of their having or not having slaves. These two causes," he explained, "concurred in forming the great division of interests in the U[nited] States. It did not lie between the large & small States: It lay between the Northern & Southern, and if any defensive power were necessary, it ought to be mutually given to these two interests." In an interesting aside that has not been much emphasized by historians, Madison went on to propose a bicameral legislative system in which one house would represent only the free people, an arrangement, he pointed out, that would give "the Southern Scale . . . the advantage in one House, and the Northern in the other."[16]

No other delegate seems to have picked up on this particular proposal, but Madison's analysis of "the great division of interests" obviously struck deep resonances among the delegates. If a few delegates explicitly lamented with Pennsylvania delegate Gouverneur Morris that an invidious "distinction had been set up & urged, between the No[rthern] and Southern States,"[17] several others reiterated Madison's views that, in the words of Rufus King of Massachusetts, the "difference of interests did not lie where it had hitherto been discussed between the great & small States; but between the Southern & Eastern"[18] and that the critical variable in accounting for that difference was the presence of large-scale racial slavery in the southern states, what George Mason referred to as that "peculiar species of property, over & above the other species of property common to all the States."[19] Already by July 14, 1787, Madison could observe without fear of contradiction that it "seemed now to be pretty well understood that the real difference of interests [in the Union] lay . . . between the N[orthern] & South[er]n States" and that the "institution of slavery & its consequences formed the line of discrimination."[20]

There was considerably less agreement over where to draw the line between those two great interests. That Georgia, South Carolina, and North Carolina fell within the southern interest while the four New England states, New York, and New Jersey fell within the northern interest seemed clear, albeit both New Jersey and New York still had significant numbers of slaves. Where Pennsylvania, Delaware, Maryland and Virginia belonged was far less obvious. Madison and many others drew the line at the Maryland-Pennsylvania border,[21] but Jonathan Dayton of New Jersey argued that Pennsylvania was a swing state and included Delaware among the southern states,[22] while Charles Coatesworth Pinckney of South Carolina found it necessary to insist that Virginia ought to be considered "a Southern State."[23]

Once it had been so widely articulated and sanctioned by solemn discussion in the Philadelphia Convention, the conception of the American Union as a potentially fragile amalgam between distinctive northern and southern interests could scarcely fail to inform discussions over the merits of the new Constitution. Many leaders, perhaps those who were most deeply committed to perpetuating the union that had guided the republic through a long and successful war for independence, denounced the tendency to view national political life in such terms. They decried the climate of sectional jealousy and suspicion that both supported and perpetuated that tendency and stressed the mutuality of interests between the productive states of the south and the carrying states of the north, between states made strong by their large populations of free people and those rendered weak by their numerous slaves. With Archibald Maclaine of the North Carolina ratifying convention, they denied that "the interests of the states" were "so dissimilar" and argued that the states were "all nearly alike, and inseparably connected."[24] Still others resisted the tendency to conflate complex regional differences "in soil, climate, customs, produce, and every thing" into two discrete and antagonistic interests and continued to think in terms of a tripartite division among the "Eastern, Southern, and . . . Middle States."[25]

Notwithstanding the efforts of such people, opinion leaders among both the pro- and anti-Constitution forces persisted in thinking in terms of a broad north-south split in the union. In extensive discussions in the press, in correspondence, in legislative chambers, and in the ratifying conventions, people often referred to—and thereby gave credence and legitimacy to—the idea that, in the words of James Iredell of North Carolina, the union was divided into "what is called the northern and southern interests."[26] Even when they admitted that the "pursuits, habits, and principles" of the "Eastern States" were "essentially different from those of [both] the Middle and Southern States," they often avowed, as did Charles Pinckney in the South Carolina ratifying convention, that, however great the differences between the eastern and middle states might be, they were by no means so "striking" as those between the two northern sections, on the one hand, and the southern, on the other. "Nature," said Pinckney, in elaborating what was rapidly becoming conventional wisdom, "has drawn as strong marks of distinction in the habits and manners of the people as she has in her climate and productions. The southern citizen beholds, with a kind of surprise, the simple manners of the east . . . while they, in their turn, seem concerned at what they term the extravagance and dissipation of their southern friends, and reprobate, as unpardonable moral and political evil, the dominion they hold over part of the human race."[27]

As Pinckney's remark reveals, while American political leaders during the struggle over the Constitution were coming to define national political life in terms of a broad north-south division, they were also defining that division mostly in terms of the extent and depth of the commitment to slavery. In Europe as well as in all parts of America during the 1780s, the conviction that slavery was a moral outrage and incompatible with civilized life was still relatively new and by no means commanded widespread acceptance in the public world. The great revolution in sentiment on this issue, perhaps the most profound and most astonishing revolution that occurred during the late eighteenth century, was yet at about midpoint in its development. As late as 1770, slavery was an expanding institution in all of Britain's continental American colonies except Nova Scotia, New Hampshire, and Canada, and, as the New York lawyer John Jay subsequently remarked, "the great majority" of Americans manifested no hostility to slavery, "very few of them even" doubting "the propriety and rectitude of it."[28]

But the Revolution had put slavery on the road to extinction in

all states in which it had limited economic utility. By the late 1780s
only Delaware, New Jersey, and New York among the northern
states still had large numbers of slaves, [29] and there was a growing
feeling, even among many large slave holders of the Upper South,
that, as Maryland delegate Luther Martin suggested in the Philadelphia Convention, any encouragement of slavery "was inconsistent with the principles of the revolution and dishonorable to the
American character." [30] For the first time in the national arena,
debate over the appropriate formula for taxing and representing
slaves and the abolition of the slave trade produced a vigorous and
extensive exchange over the institution of slavery. Delegates from
the Middle states and the Upper South, in particular Gouverneur
Morris and George Mason, unequivocally denounced slavery and
its social effects, Morris contrasting "the free regions of the Middle
States, where a rich & noble cultivation marks the prosperity &
happiness of the people, with the misery & poverty which over-
spread the barren wastes of V[irgini]a Mary[lan]d & the other
States having slaves" [31] and Mason decrying the "pernicious" influence of slavery on arts, manufactures, and manners and predicting
that it would in time "bring the judgment of heaven on" the
"Country." [32] The states these men represented—Pennsylvania
and Virginia—were also the most insistent upon putting an immediate end to the slave trade.

The defense of slavery in the Convention came entirely from
delegates from the Lower South, with the South Carolinians
taking the lead. Threatening to leave the union if the slave trade
were not permitted to continue for a limited time, they argued
that, at least for the immediate future, South Carolina and Georgia
could not "do without slaves." John Rutledge declared that "Religion & humanity had nothing to do with the question," while
Charles Pinckney "cited the case of Greece and Rome & other
antient States" as well as "the sanction given by France[,] England, Holland & other modern States" to support his argument
that, so far from being "wrong," slavery was "justified by the

example of all the world," "one half" of which "in all ages" had "been slaves."[33]

Notwithstanding the vow of secrecy that bound the Convention, echoes, even direct paraphrases, of these discussions could be heard in the ensuing debate over the Constitution. Rumors spread through the southern states that northerners wanted to do away with not merely the slave trade but slavery itself. "It is well known to have been the intention of the Eastern and Northern States to abolish slavery altogether when [they had it] in their power," Lachlan McIntosh of Georgia wrote to a correspondent in late 1787,[34] and in all of the southern ratifying conventions for which records of debate survive, in South Carolina, Virginia, and North Carolina, Antifederalists charged that adoption of the Constitution would lead eventually to the destruction of slavery. In South Carolina Rawlins Lowndes expressed alarm that "Without negroes, this state would degenerate into one of the most contemptible in the Union" and vigorously defended slavery "on the principles of religion, humanity, and justice."[35] No one came forward with a positive defense of slavery in Virginia, but both Patrick Henry and George Mason were fearful that the national government would eventually act against slavery and argued that "prudence" forbade its abolition.[36]

To allay these fears, Federalists found themselves driven to assure their audiences, as they had done with reference to so many contested elements in the Constitution, that, as Madison put it, the "general government" had only delegated powers and that those powers did not include authority "to interpose with respect to the property in slaves now held by the states."[37] Thus, while acknowledging his agreement with Lowndes "that the nature of our climate, and the flat, swampy situation of our country, obliges us to cultivate our lands with negroes, and that without them South Carolina would soon be a desert waste," C. C. Pinckney insisted that the failure of the Constitution expressly to grant the national government power to emancipate slaves provided ample

security that it would never do so.[38] At no point during the
Philadelphia Convention, Edmund Randolph told the Virginia
Convention, had "the *Southern States, even South Carolina her-
self* . . . had *the smallest suspicion of an abolition of slavery.*"[39]

### III

If the debate over the Constitution contributed to the widespread
articulation and circulation of an enhanced sense of potential tensions between the northern and the southern states, a heightened
awareness of the controversial nature of slavery, and perhaps even a
fuller comprehension among southerners of the cultural similarities that linked them together in opposition to the middle and
New England states, it did not witness the emergence of an all
subsuming southern identity. As David Potter has reminded us,
recognition of social and "cultural similarities alone will not provide a basis of affinity between groups." Nationalism and similar
collective loyalties have to rest on "*two* psychological bases": an
awareness "of a common culture *and* the feeling of common interest." "Of the two," he posits, "the concept of culture is, no doubt, of
greater weight," but it cannot have its full effect without a mutual
awareness of common interests.[40]

That the southern states did not yet have an overriding sense of a
common interest can be seen by the divisions among them over
both the slave trade and slavery. Even if they could not see any way
to abolish slavery, many Virginians, both among the delegation to
the Philadelphia Convention and in the Virginia ratifying convention, condemned slavery and militantly opposed the slave trade.
South Carolinians and Georgians, on the other hand, insisted on
not closing the slave trade, candidly admitted the utility of slavery
to the economy of the Lower South, and, in a few cases, even
defended slavery in positive terms. In North Carolina there were
political leaders who subscribed to each of these views.[41]

In Philadelphia, even their common interest as staple-exporting
states in keeping foreign trade open and unencumbered could not

override their disagreements over the slave trade. Rather than forming a united front on issues involving commercial regulations, the Lower Southern states aligned themselves with New England in a well-known bargain, opposed by the Upper South, by which the Lower South agreed to endow the federal government with authority to enact navigation laws while New Englanders consented not to empower it to close the slave trade for twenty years.[42]

Indeed, a close look at Forrest McDonald's table on voting compatibility among the states in the Federal Convention quickly reveals that the southern states demonstrated relatively little voting cohesion. North Carolina, South Carolina, and Georgia all voted together rather consistently (more than 65% of the time). Although Virginia voted often with North Carolina, it voted far more frequently with Pennsylvania and Massachusetts than it did with either Georgia or South Carolina. To the extent that there was a southern voting bloc Maryland was not a part of it. Although Maryland sided with Virginia almost as often as it did with Delaware, it voted less with South Carolina than with any other state and less with North Carolina than with any of the other states except New York and South Carolina.[43] These findings have more recently been confirmed by Calvin H. Jillson and Cecil L. Eubanks in their illuminating analysis of voting patterns in the Convention. They depict a broad division not between northern states and southern states but between a liberal, expansive central core and a more parochial and locally-oriented periphery. Though this pattern by no means held on all issues, it clearly placed Virginia closer to the middle states, especially to Pennsylvania, than to the states of the Lower South.[44]

However much leaders of the southern states may have come to think of themselves as part of a broad southern, slaveholding interest during the revolutionary era, many Virginians, as evidenced both by their voting behavior and by their explicit declarations, clearly regarded Virginia more as a "central" than as a southern state. George Washington was by no means the only prominent Virginian who referred to the Carolinas and Georgia as the "Southern states" and classified Virginia as one of "the middle states."[45] Not just because of its "central situation" geographically within the union but also because of its size, wealth, and conspicuous leadership in most of the major events associated with the Revolution and foundation of the American nation, Washington and others thought of Virginia as being "at the centre of the states." Well aware that Virginia was one of the "commanding" states of the union and admirably situated in terms of its location to preside over and reap large benefits from the westward and southwestward expansion of population into Kentucky, Tennessee, and the Ohio country, they automatically assumed that it would have a defining role in the new union and had no intention of permitting it to be shunted off into a marginal position.[46]

This was precisely the sort of leadership role Virginia had assumed at the Philadelphia Convention. George Washington was the unanimous choice of the delegates to preside; Edmund Randolph introduced the plan that formed the basis for early discussions; and James Madison contributed so heavily to the discussions that he has often been referred to as the father of the Constitution. A tally of Madison's notes reveals that Madison, George Mason, and Randolph were all among the ten most frequent participants in the debates, Madison being exceeded in this regard only by Gouverneur Morris, and Mason only by Morris, Madison, and James Wilson. Together, Virginia's seven delegates accounted for just over 19% of Convention interventions, just a fraction of a percentage point below the figure for Pennsylvania's eight delegates.

In 1787–88, Virginians had no reason to think that Virginia's contribution to the new union might be any less conspicuous, and in the short run, of course, they were correct. Supplying four of the first five presidents, the most prominent chief justice of the Supreme Court, and a large number of congressional leaders, Virginia did indeed play a key part in the formation of the federal union. Only after its rapid decline in prestige and power after 1815 had deprived Virginia of its central place did it slowly drift into a closer emotional association with the rest of the southern states and itself begin to become more self-consciously southern.[47]

To describe Virginia's role as central in 1787–88 is by no means to suggest that that of the other southern states was marginal. Georgia, which was scarcely more than a half-century old, and North Carolina still had relatively undeveloped and small leadership pools and played a less prominent part in the Convention. But the four delegates from South Carolina, the state with the highest per capita wealth in the Revolutionary generation, were far from invisible. Charles Pinckney ranked seventh among all delegates in terms of frequency of participation in the debates, while John Rutledge ranked twelfth, Pierce Butler fourteenth, and C. C. Pinckney seventeenth. Only the delegates from the three largest states, Pennsylvania, Virginia, and Massachusetts, had more interventions, the four South Carolina delegates accounting for 14% of the total, just a fraction less than the four Massachusetts delegates and well above Connecticut, whose delegates were responsible for just over 11% of interventions. Eighth on the list, Hugh Williamson was the only delegate from North Carolina to rank among the twenty-five most frequent participants. With 6% of the interventions, however, the North Carolina delegation slightly exceeded the contributions of those from Delaware and Maryland and was way ahead of those from New York, New Jersey, New Hampshire and Georgia. At seventeenth, Luther Martin was the only Marylander to be in the top twenty participants, and no Georgian appeared in the top thirty.

In contrast to Virginia the states of the Lower South neither played such a conspicuous part in the constitutional revolution of 1787–88 nor aspired to such a prominent role in the union, but it is important to emphasize that they all were highly optimistic about their respective futures during the founding era. For several decades, South Carolina and Georgia had had the highest value of exports per capita of any state in the Union, and in recent decades only New Hampshire had matched those two states and North

Carolina in terms of their rates of white population growth. Between 1750 and 1780, the white population of Georgia had increased more than seven times, that of North Carolina by 237%,
and that of South Carolina by 232%. These figures are somewhat
higher than those for New Hampshire at 224% and well ahead of
any found for the same period in the other states to the north,
among which New York with 188%, Pennsylvania with 174%, and
Virginia with 145% were the leaders. Over the same period, the
slave populations, to some extent still a reflection of buying power,
also rose rapidly, that of Georgia increasing almost twenty times,
that of North Carolina by 360%, and that of South Carolina at
149%, a figure just below Virginia's 154%.[48]

A substantial part of the astonishing white population growth
among the Lower Southern states was, like that for Virginia, the
result of immigration from the northern states. Both because most
"of the Northern States," as Edward Rutledge of South Carolina
declared during the debate over whether to refer the Constitution
to a ratifying convention, "were already full of people," because
"the migrations to the south were immense," and because the
southern states all had "great quantity of lands still uncultivated,"
it seemed evident, as Pierce Butler announced in the Philadelphia
Convention, that the "people & strength of America" were "evidently bearing Southwardly & S[outh] westw[ar]dly" and that the
southern states, including Virginia, would soon "predominate"
over what one North Carolina delegate referred to as the "small,
pitiful states to the north." The rapid growth of Kentucky and
Tennessee in the late 1770s and 1780s seemed to provide additional
testimony for the legitimacy of these expectations. Within a half
century, predicted David Ramsay of South Carolina, the southern
states could scarcely fail to have "a great ascendancy over the
Eastern."[49]

In the final analysis, of course, all of the southern states acted in
the struggle over the Constitution in a way a majority of their
leaders thought best in terms of their interests and conceptions of
their own goals and priorities not as a part of the south but as

separate and mostly long-established corporate entities, each with a long history and a clearly understood sense of its own potentialities and weaknesses in the situation in which it then found itself. "Each State like each individual," Connecticut delegate Roger Sherman told his colleagues in Philadelphia, "had its peculiar habits, usages and manners, which constituted its happiness." In these early days of nationhood and national community formation, loyalties to these state interests and identities still took precedence over sectional considerations.[50]

The tendency to think in terms of state or even national rather than sectional considerations was reinforced by mutual suspicions and hostilities among states. Southerners were skeptical not only about northerners but about each other. South Carolinians regarded Virginian attitudes on slavery and the slave trade as "interested and inconsistent,"[51] C. C. Pinckney pointing out in the Philadelphia Convention that because Virginia had more slaves than it needed it would actually "gain by stopping the importations" and thereby raising the value of their surplus slaves.[52] Virginians looked askance at their weaker and less prominent southern neighbors, Patrick Henry describing North Carolina as "a *poor, despised place*," and William Grayson suggesting that South Carolinians still went abroad "mounted on alligators."[53]

## IV

If there was a growing awareness in the southern states during the late Revolutionary era of a broad southern interest and of the extent to which a strong commitment to slavery defined that interest, the southern states in 1787–88 did not yet constitute a cohesive sectional unit. The states of the Upper South, especially Virginia, had quite different attitudes towards slavery and the slave trade and a different conception of their relationship to the Union than did the states of the Lower South. Partly because antislavery sentiment was still relatively new and relatively limited, partly because the process of abolition had not yet even begun in the

northern states of New York and New Jersey, and partly because
northerners had not yet attacked slavery in the southern states,
slavery was by no means as important either as a point of sectional
differentiation or as a social and political issue as it would become
after 1830 or even after 1820, and its potentially disruptive effects
were by no means so clear as they would be by 1820.

Similarly, population growth among the southern states, the
spread of slavery into Kentucky and Tennessee, and the expan-
siveness to which those developments gave rise inhibited the
emergence of the idea that the southern slave interest might be a
permanent minority interest within the union. Nor had explicit
sectional politics yet come into play in the national arena. New
Englanders had not yet retreated into that "unbending Federalism
that would later set" their region "at odds with the rest of the
nation" and especially with southern republicans.[54] The militantly
agrarian minority of southern republicans had not yet formulated
their defensive states-rights and narrow-constructionist political
position.[55]

Indeed, the prominence of the southern states in the major
events of the Revolution as well as in the formation of the Federal
Constitution and the establishment and early years of the American republic clearly reveals that their inhabitants had not yet
come to be thought of by people from other areas or to think of
themselves as being in the center of American political culture.

With the phased abolition of slavery in the British Empire and
the spread of disdain for slavery throughout the northern areas of
the United States after 1820, the southern states' continuing commitment to a slave labor system resulted in a growing divergence
between their patterns of social organization and values and those
of the increasingly urban and industrialized societies of the north.
In their obvious "hierarchy, the cult of chivalry—the unmachined
civilization, the folk society, the rural values," the southern states,
as Potter has argued, seemed to have acquired a "*distinctiveness* of
a deeply significant kind," one that was both less and less con-

gruent with the social character and orientation of the states to the north and out of step with the rest of the civilized world. Notwithstanding their economic origins, the southern states seemed to have developed "a climate that was uncongenial" to the capitalist spirit that still thrived in the north.[56]

From the perspective of these developments, the divergencies among the southern and northern states during the Revolutionary era would appear in retrospect by 1850 and 1861 to have been latently significant. From the immediate perspective of their common experience in mounting and carrying out a successful war for independent nationhood, however, their commonalities probably seemed much more impressive than their differences and gave credence to the widely held hope that all the states were part of "a common culture that transcended sectional differences." Few could have found incredible Washington's assertion in his Farewell Address in 1796 that "with slight shades of difference" Americans had "the same religion, manners, habits and political principles."[57] Insofar as it already existed, however, southern *distinctiveness* did not appear to be of overriding importance to most members of the Revolutionary generation in either the northern or the southern states. The development of a powerful, self-conscious, slavery-conscious sectionalism lay ahead, primarily in the years after 1820.

# Natural Rights, Bills of Rights, and the People's Rights in Virginia Constitutional Discourse, 1787–1791

DAVID THOMAS KONIG

Perhaps it was appropriate that Virginians, who took the lead in propelling the colonies toward independence in 1776, would also take the lead in moving the newly independent states toward revolutionary political reform in 1787. Perhaps it was appropriate, too, that Virginians would reflect the national divisions over the Constitution by dividing sharply among and within themselves over the new plan. Caught in the welter of ambiguities that the Constitution exposed in their thinking between 1787 and 1791, Virginians found themselves in an agonizing struggle over the very meaning of government. So deep and tangled were the conflicting strands of political thought that they plunged one of America's most unified and stable political elites into open conflict; indeed, the need to devise specific practical forms for shared, unspoken ideas not only divided Virginians against each other, but it also divided individuals against themselves, as the debates forced them to reassess and even doubt many ideas that they had held without question throughout their political lives. To reconcile these differences, Virginians struggled at the federal constitutional convention in Philadelphia, at the Confederation Congress meeting in Philadelphia, and then at the state ratifying convention in Richmond. Their divisions, and their efforts to reconcile them, however, did not cease with ratification. Several Virginians con-

tinued to lobby for a second constitutional convention to consider
major amendments to the Constitution, and they came close to
achieving their wish when the First Congress, meeting in the
unfinished former city hall of New York, dealt with the lists of
amendments that Virginia and other states had proposed as a Bill of
Rights. Yet the struggle did not end there, either. Virginians at the
First Congress also took the lead in drafting the first federal
statutes that would implement and give meaning to the skeletal
constitutional framework set up. Only then did they achieve the
workable form suitable to their ideas.

The divisions that informed these efforts centered on ambiguities that have characterized the South to this day. The conflict
would produce what has been called, aptly enough, an "ambivalent legacy," a term that expresses the uncertain coexistence of a
strong regional identity within the shared identity of a larger
national sphere.[1] But this legacy was bequeathed long before the
1780s; it was, rather, a bequest left to Virginians by their colonial
ancestors.

It is important to establish the very early origins of this intertwined identity of regionalism within nationalism. To do so, however, requires us to revise our image of Virginia's political leaders
in the late eighteenth century. We know they disagreed with one
another, but it is not easy to accept the fact that these men did not
come to Philadelphia with fully worked out ideas from which they
retreated only reluctantly as discrete, practical concessions to
political compromise. On the contrary, it must be recognized that
genuine uncertainty beset them—even the well prepared James
Madison and the astute George Mason. To do so, however, requires us to acknowledge the fallibility of men whom Jefferson has
led us to treat, in his words, as an "assembly of demigods." But
Jefferson, we must recall, did not attend the Philadelphia or
Richmond conventions. George Mason, who did, warned a throng
of voters at the Fairfax County Courthouse to regard the Philadelphia framers skeptically. Urging them to elect Antifederalist
delegates to the state ratifying convention at Richmond, he re-

called his own perceptions of those who had drafted the Constitution at Philadelphia: "You may have been taught . . . to respect the Characters of the Members of the late Convention. You may have supposed that they were an assemblage of great men. There is nothing less true."

Publicly, he did not include his fellow Virginians in the group he labelled "Knaves and Fools," "Coxcombs" and "officehunters."[2] Privately, bewilderment and criticism of fellow Virginians flow undiluted through the correspondence of the state's political leaders on both sides of the ratification issue and then in equally intense form over the Bill of Rights. Madison, for example, confessed to Washington in September 1787 that he was "at some loss to comprehend" how the otherwise perceptive Mason could so badly misinterpret the Constitution's judiciary provision (Article III).[3] A month later he reflected on the Richmond debates, "The diversity of opinion on so interesting a subject among men of equal integrity & discernment is at once a melancholy proof of the fallibility of the human judgement and of the imperfect progress yet made in the Science of government."[4]

That same month Edward Carrington, whose support for a strong central government had led Powhatan County electors to reject his candidacy for a seat at the Richmond convention, noted how the Antifederalists agreed on little beyond their opposition to ratification. "[T]he disapprobation of Mr. R. H. L[ee] and that of Mr. G[rayson] are founded on very opposite principles—the former thinks the Constitution too strong, the latter is of the opinion that it is too weak."[5] Carrington, writing from Congress, was reporting on the continued divisions among Virginians there. Henry Lee and Richard Henry Lee, Grayson and Carrington, could achieve no common ground on the practical implementation of government. The division, Carrington observed, was merely "the same schism which unfortunately happened in our State in Philadelphia, [and it] threatens us here also."[6] The twistings of Governor Edmund Randolph remain epiphenomenal. After presenting the centralizing scheme known as the Virginia Plan, Randolph refused to sign the Constitution at Philadelphia but then shocked fellow Virginians by arguing for its ratification at Richmond. An infuriated Patrick Henry was unable to explain Randolph's second about-face or to understand the ambivalences that plagued the governor. "It seems very strange and unaccountable," hinted Henry at the Richmond debates, "that that which was the object of his execration should now receive his encomiums. Something extraordinary must have operated so great a change in his opinion."[7] Worthy of being labelled a latter-day Hamlet, Randolph suffered the insult of being labelled, instead, a latter-day Benedict Arnold by George Mason.[8]

These uncertainties and turnabouts reflect more than the convenient realignments of politicians. They also reflect more than a simple disagreement over state's rights. State's rights certainly were one manifestation of the debate, but at bottom these uncertainties and reversals reflected, simultaneously, a consensus on rights but an imperfectly worked out notion of how best to establish them through practical provisions. *That* assertion will not surprise many historians, but it is a proposition that requires us to break new ground in understanding exactly what institutional arrangements Virginians had come to rely upon for protecting their rights in the eighteenth century. And that is a much more difficult question. Once we can answer it, however, we will have gone a great distance toward understanding the fundamental concepts of Southern legal and constitutional thought, and thereby the substructure of debate that divided Virginians from 1787 to 1791.

The question of rights dominated political discourse in Virginia no less than it did in other states. Virginians, like most of their counterparts in the other new states, took great pains to assure the rights upon which they went to war. As a result Virginians on June 12, 1776, adopted George Mason's draft of a "Declaration of Rights." The impact of this document, so important to Virginians in the eighteenth century, is nonetheless open to question when we turn to the federal Constitution. If anything, Mason's Declaration is another sort of "ambivalent legacy" that characterizes the Southern legal tradition. It is ambivalent for at least two reasons.

In large part, the legacy of Mason's Declaration is ambivalent because the list was *not* part of Virginia's own Constitution. John Marshall, who would leave an indelible imprint on the federal Constitution by way of more than three decades of interpretation as Chief Justice of the Supreme Court, made this point very clearly at the Richmond ratification debates two hundred years ago, and it is worth repeating. Addressing the repeated and insistent predictions that the federal Constitution would not protect jury trials without a bill of rights, Marshall asked if the *Virginia* constitution so provided. "Does our Constitution direct trials to be by jury? It is required in our bill of rights, which is not part of the Constitution of 1776." Marshall was absolutely right. The Virginia Constitution of 1776 included the Declaration of Independence as well as Mason's Declaration of Rights, and generally adapted the colonial charter to republicanism by making its governor and upper house of the legislature elective. Beyond that, it did nothing to solve the fundamental constitutional problem that had led to the War for Independence: namely, the protection of liberty from power. In the Commonwealth of Virginia, Marshall lectured his unwilling pupils at the suitably named New Academy building, "The Bill of Rights is merely recommendatory."[9]

Marshall's point, if not well taken by listeners at the New Academy building, merits our scrutiny and respect here for it suggests the other reason for ambivalence. The Virginia Bill of Rights was a statement by a sovereign state with inherent—*not delegated*—powers. Like King-in Parliament, the Virginia assembly was the sovereign power of the state, restrained only by those notions of justice that could not be violated by statute. Such was the "natural rights" dimension that Englishmen proudly attributed to their constitution. Parliament could not (or, more precisely, should not and thus *would not*) violate such principles— whatever they were. But just how did Mason's Declaration of natural law principles protect such rights in practice? It provides, in truth, only exhortation. Its sixteen provisions state the "basis and foundation of government" but speak in only precatory—not mandatory—terms. For example, "all Power of suspending Laws by any Authority without consent of the Representatives of the people is injurious to their rights and *ought* not to be exercised." When John Marshall referred to jury trial, he was citing provision number 11, which stated that in civil suits "the antient Trial by Jury is *preferable* to any other and *ought* to be held sacred." These provisions speak "ought," not "must" or "shall," and they reveal how the Virginia Bill of Rights is a set of principles and obligations ("maxims," as Virginians called them) and not of commands or immoveable barriers.[10] This is, of course, perfectly in keeping with a sovereign state whose powers are inherent and extensive, not delegated and narrow. These rights are qualifiable; that is, they are subject to legislative reinterpretation and abridgement.[11] That Mason conceived of a bill of rights in this manner is not surprising: it was orthodoxy in Anglo-American constitutional theory and reflected the very same wording of the English Bill of Rights.[12] To be truly meaningful and secure, natural rights required not exhortation, but such limitations that only statutory enactment could provide—and, conversely, that statutory enactment could turn around and someday violate. Patrick Henry's opposition to the Constitution, when he argued its failure to provide explicit guarantees of basic rights, therefore did not impress Governor Edmund Randolph, who reminded Henry of the Virginia assembly's own conviction and execution by legislative attainder of one Josiah Phillips, in open defiance of the commonwealth's enshrinement of trial by jury. "Was this arbitrary deprivation of life, the dearest gift of God to man, consistent with the genius of republican government?" Randolph demanded. Henry could only reply, as he did so often to those who pointed out his inconsistency, that the law of nature *had been* followed, since the assembly had acted out of necessity, which he called "the law of nature and nations."[13]

If natural law was proving irrelevant to the hard political reality of drafting a national framework of government, it already had proved so in arguments for and against slavery. Numerous Virginians opposed the system and, among other arguments, attacked it as a violation of divine and natural law. At the same time, others used the natural law argument as a defense of slavery; the two views even confronted each other in particular freedom cases heard by Virginia courts, whose judges studiously avoided addressing the question and always decided slave freedom cases on more technically procedural or statutory points, or according to basic common law principles governing chattel property or inheritance.[14] Jefferson pleaded natural law in freedom cases he argued for particular slaves, but other lawyers could use it with equal vehemence to justify slavery; they might even cite the very same chapter from Pufendorf's natural law treatise that Jefferson used against slavery.[15] Moreover, Jefferson could not deny the widespread natural law insistence on the right to property as well as its corollary, the natural right to free trade.[16] Even if he had been able to establish the supremacy of a slave's natural right to property, Jefferson had to admit that natural law without statutory implementation was largely useless. When Virginians drafted their state constitution in 1776 he had admitted that Virginians were "free to declare" a law to be "an infringement of natural right" but powerless to do anything about it without statutory enactment.[17] On the immediate and pressing practical matter of slavery, therefore, natural law had little jurisprudential meaning, whether adjudicated in a state court or federal tribunal.[18]

Slavery, then, posed more of an academic dilemma for natural rights theorists than it did for the framers or ratifiers of the Convention. Despite James Madison's famous statement that it would be "wrong to admit in the Constitution the idea that there could be property in men,"[19] not even the most ardent Federalist or abolitionist believed that government under the Federal Constitution would abolish slavery. "Let me ask, if they should even attempt it," Edmund Randolph assured the Richmond convention, "if it will not be a usurpation of power. There is no power to warrant it, in that paper. If there be, I know it not."[20] Randolph gave an enormous amount of thought to the Constitution and to the dangers it might have embodied—to *every* danger indeed, as he tore himself from support to opposition and back to support. But I am sure that he was speaking truly when he confessed that he did not think that the abolition of slavery was one of them.

Virginia's problems with the Constitution went far deeper than the preservation of slavery. Rather, they went deep into the ambivalence of recognizing the manifest need for a national system powerful enough to assert a "supreme law of the land" against wayward local judiciaries while at the same time conceding the general efficacy of local justice. Put differently, they saw threats and protections in each jurisdiction. To an anonymous correspondent in the *Virginia Independent Chronicle* over two hundred years ago, the question was

> Whether, it is, not more likely that the blaze of LIBERTY will be kept alive among us, when watched on thirteen separate Altars, than when re-united into one, be it ever so refulgent.[21]

Those who opposed the Constitution had serious misgivings about the actual institutional arrangements submitted to them in the summer of 1788, misgivings that divided them from one another as sharply as they set them off from those who supported it. James Madison, for example, wrote to George Washington just before Virginia delegates assembled at Richmond and reported that already Henry and Mason "appeared to take different and weak ground" in their opposition to the new government.[22] In the next four weeks, their opposition would divide them still further, and would drive them onto weaker ground yet.

What *did* the Virginians agree on? Enough of them, 89 out of 168, agreed to ratify the Constitution, but they did so with a qualification—not a legal condition, that is, but the political demand that a Bill of Rights be added to the document. Yet there, too, agreement seems to have had its limits. Virginians had their own "Bill of Rights," but its text began by referring to itself as a "declaration of rights." The distinction is not semantic, but reveals a deep uncertainty about what such a document meant. As a state document, its language is precatory, filled with "ought" rather than "shall." Henry Lee, a nationalist who saw little need and only great danger in enumerating rights in this manner, cautioned that such a bill started Virginians down a slippery slope toward omnipotent government. The Virginia Bill of Rights reflected an understanding by which, Lee explained, "the people reserve to themselves certain enumerated rights, and . . . the rest were vested in their rulers; . . . consequently, the powers reserved to the people were but an inconsiderable exception from what were given to their ruler."[23] If Virginians were to insist upon a similar document for the new federal government, would they not be granting the very type of consolidating national authority that they so vehemently argued against? Indeed they would. How could Virginians argue simultaneously for a limited government of delegated powers and at the same time insist on a declaration of rights that derived from notions of sovereignty based on a government of inherent and ultimately limitless powers?

What were Virginians to do? Ironically, those most opposed to a central, consolidated government argued for a Bill of Rights that implicitly accepted the notion of the very thing they so vehemently opposed. Those who sought a more powerful national government argued with equal irony that the new framework established only a federated union possessing specifically delegated powers. These men, led by Madison, Edmund Pendleton, George Nicholas, and George Wythe, had to point out to their opponents that a bill of rights was superfluous in such a government. Madison recalled the long tradition of reluctance in Anglo-American law to place precise and express limitations on government. Ever since the Parliamentary discussion of the 1620s, when wary opponents of the Stuarts warned that an enumeration of "particular" rights would "rather contract than enlarge" rights, opponents of tyrannical government had shied away from the attempt. Madison reminded his opponents of what they were saying, and even had to caution other Federalists that "an imperfect enumeration is dangerous." Challenging those who demanded a Bill of Rights, Madison asked, "If an enumeration be made of our rights, will it not be implied that every thing omitted is given to the general government?"[24] Maybe so, replied one writer in the *Virginia Independent Chronicle:* the Constitution was not establishing a general government with inherent powers, but someday that government would *become* so, and therefore a bill of rights was needed.[25]

But what sort of bill of rights would it be? Precatory maxims in the language of "ought" granted, by implication, an inherently sovereign and ultimately illimitable national government. Express reservations were superfluous to a government of delegated powers and implied that the national government possessed all nonenumerated rights. Which implied danger was greater, and which language might be relied on, accordingly, to assure rights?

Given their uncertainty, Virginians not surprisingly used both sorts of language. When they finished their work at Richmond, the delegates sent *two* lists of amendments to the new Congress. And what lists they were: two lists of twenty suggestions each. The first, referred to as "a declaration or bill of rights" (they still could not decide which) proposed precatory maxims based on Mason's Declaration of Rights, while the second, referred to as "amendments to the Constitution," contained express limitations and exceptions to delegated federal powers.[26]

Why not decide between the two? Why, indeed, even ratify the Constitution, if it would lead to such a government? In large part, the point was moot: Maryland, to the north, already had ratified when the Virginia delegates assembled at Richmond, and two days into the convention they received word that South Carolina had ratified. But the delegates might have followed Jefferson's suggestion, which Patrick Henry supported, that Virginia hold out even after nine states had joined the union, as leverage to assure ratification of a Bill of Rights. But it all goes beyond such considerations of political strategy and touches, rather, the Virginians' shared but imperfectly developed notion of bills of rights.

Their ambivalence suggests that the emotional debates over the Constitution were so deep and emotional precisely because they originated from a deeply held consensus. Did Virginians disagree so sharply precisely because they agreed on so much in the first place? I submit that this was the case. That is, Virginians agreed on their legacy of constitutionalism as firmly as they disagreed on the future of the Constitution.

I think so because, for one thing, common language and concerns recur throughout the debates among men who took opposing positions on ratification. Even metaphor recurs among opponents and begs explanation: George Mason's boast that "he would sooner chop off his right hand than put it to the Constitution as it now stands" was based on the same common fund of political discourse as Edmund Randolph's assertion that he would "assent to the lopping off of this limb [as he pointed to his arm] before I assent to the dissolution of the Union" through a refusal to ratify.[27] And, once Virginians would agree on The Bill of Rights, their agreement would resonate, too. Madison's speech in Congress for such a bill of rights "to satisfy the public" echoed Mason's call for it as a way to "give great quiet to the people"; Madison thought the task would require "but one day," Mason a few hours.[28] The shared political language reveals more than form; it touches, too, the substance of a fundamental unity and consensus on the meaning of constitutionalism.

Throughout the Richmond debates a single thread is woven—a recurring theme in general, with a recurring specific concern. The concern is the reliance on local institutions to preserve a larger conception of rights. These were not state's rights, but the right to a body of justice that protects the liberty and property of the community. Virginians sought to preserve, not local self-interest or prejudice, but a notion of rights and justice that depended on what Madison called "communion of interests and sympathy of sentiments" among a community. But such rights, as the turmoil of the Confederation had revealed, might require reinforcement through the operation of a "constitution paramount to the government."[29] In colonial Virginia, this had taken the form of a balance between the locality and provincial institutions that could not be easily reduced to iron rules or express wording. Colonial Virginians, that is, had developed a system of justice based on locally determined rules and substantive concepts which suited the variety of parochial needs and understanding and were implemented by local men, but which operated within a centrally enforced structure of due process jurisprudence.[30]

For Virginians in the Early Republic, justice was local justice, a system in which the facts and even law were determined by local juries, presided over by local judges familiar with the norms and expectations of a locality. At the same time, for Virginians in the Early Republic justice meant adherence to due process and the need for some superior power to intervene when "a particular interest" corrupted the system and frustrated the impartiality and honesty upon which republicanism depend. Legislatively, this concept explains not only Mason's Antifederalism but also his simultaneous call for a stronger Congress with many more representatives to keep that body as closely as possible a direct reflection of local sentiments. "Sixty-five members" of Congress, he explained at Richmond, "cannot possibly know the situation and circumstances of all the inhabitants of this immense continent."[31] So, too, must the executive be strong, but of a tripartite nature in order to reflect the political sentiments of each major region.[32] If the legislature and executive were to have such power over the states, they ought to reflect local understandings. This notion also sheds light on the delicate balance that Randolph tried to achieve by introducing the Virginia plan with its Congressional intervention against unconstitutional state laws, and his subsequent ambivalence about vesting such power in appointed judges. Judicially, it gives meaning to Henry's hobby-horse of jury trial by the vicinage and helps us understand why he gave so much concern to the exact mileage that jurors might be called to travel for duty at a federal trial.[33] Only a local jury, familiar with local concepts of justice, could defend liberty and property, while only local judges and officials could implement rules and procedures of the sort that people expected and counted on for justice.

The ratification controversy did not take place within a vacuum, even within the state of Virginia. The debate usually ascribed to state rights, therefore, is actually a variant on an older struggle. If we examine closely the legal history of Virginia in this same period, we see that the constitutional discussions at Richmond were a debate writ large from struggles going on in Virginia to preserve local justice even from interference by other parts of Virginia. Two examples give an indication of this replication process. One dates from 1776, the other from 1788.

Virginia's constitution of 1776 was not enacted without rival plans. Indeed, Jefferson himself had proposed a sweeping revision of a system that he regarded as retaining too many vestiges of antirepublicanism and aristocracy. As a result, he worked with others in his home county of Albemarle to propose another constitution. All its details need not concern us here, except insofar as it, too, addressed the problem of preserving local justice and rights while at the same time remaining within the proper contours of due process. The proposed plan also posed the question of the degree to which Virginia's government was one of delegated or inherent powers. The "Albemarle County Instructions concerning the Virginia Constitution" noted the inefficacy of sweeping maxims against a tyrannical central government even if it was in Williamsburg. It, too, noted the need—and the difficulty—of drawing "a proper and clear line . . . between the powers necessary to be conferred by the Constituents to their Delegates, and what ought prudently to remain in their hands."[34] And this between a county and state government!

A dozen years later, the concern remained. Indeed, while Virginia convention delegates debated state versus federal justice, members of the Virginia Assembly also debated county versus district justice. Many men served in both bodies, and meetings of the two bodies overlapped for six weeks. In a series of letters printed in a Richmond newspaper at precisely the same time that delegates in the New Academy building offered competing ideas on how to preserve state procedures and notions of law amid a federal system, Virginians argued about protecting county courts from the encroachments of non-local courts—and not even from a central state court at Richmond, but from district courts that would amalgamate several counties. In essence, Virginians were once again debating how to preserve local judicial traditions and their institutional guarantees of rights against amalgamation by an outside force into an unfamiliar and unsympathetic larger unit.[35] This dilemma of divided and competing authority, therefore, was present at the creation of the union.

This particular debate, which in many respects replicated that over the question of a federal judiciary, had raged for three years by 1788, as Virginians argued the wisdom of creating a uniform system of law and procedure, in which local courts would be, as Pendleton called them, "different Courts which are but branches of the same Court."[36] The tumult of economic chaos in the mid-1780s had taken its toll on the venerable system of county courts that had existed in Virginia since the 1660s, and many questioned if the implicit understandings governing their law and operation were adequate to the challenges placed on them by hard-pressed creditors and debtors. The *goal* of balancing local needs and the preservation of rights remained alive and vigorous; the method of guaranteeing this had been called into question in Virginia by the vicissitudes of the 1780s.

Madison despaired of the old system and feared that it could no longer preserve that balance. Any effort to patch it together, he lamented to James Monroe, merely "demonstrated the impracticability of rendering these courts fit instruments of justice."[37] Like Pendleton and Madison, many Virginians saw a pressing need for a system of district courts that would impose a more uniform standard of justice in the new commonwealth. "I consider our county courts as on a bad footing," Madison advised Caleb

Wallace when the latter asked for advice on establishing a new government for Kentucky, "and would never myself consent to copy them into another constitution."[38] His pessimism about reforming local courts led Madison inexorably toward the creation of a level of courts with a multi-county jurisdiction, balancing local needs within a structure of law applied by more professional judges. This experience with Virginia courts, like his better known exasperation with the Virginia Assembly, would soon inform his efforts at a national government.

Virginia politics therefore had an immense impact on Madison's national politics. Indeed, it is quite likely that his defeat for the Senate—engineered by Henry's forces in the Assembly—and his near–defeat for the House after the Assembly gerrymandered his district, forced Madison to accommodate the Antifederalists' demands for a bill of rights. But Madison's shift to support of a bill of rights derived from more than the expediency of Virginia politics. Indeed, by June 1789, when he presented his ideas to the House of Representatives, Madison had come to accept much of the Antifederalist concern about consolidated government. His speech opening discussion of the Bill of Rights indicates his awareness that the federal government might, as other Virginians had warned, claim the authority of a government with inherent powers. Recanting his warning about the "dangerous" implications of a bill of rights (namely, that exceptions implied a grant of all powers not so specified) Madison argued from the Antifederalist presumption that a consolidated central government might someday emerge. Madison denied, as directly as he once had asserted, that a federal bill of rights was "dangerous" and compared it to those in state governments, which were presumed to possess inherent, residual powers. He even begins his proposed list of amendments with the precatory statement "That Government is instituted and ought to be exercised for the benefit of the people. . . ."[39] Nevertheless, Madison refused to open the way for a consolidated government of residuary powers. His amendments, like those sent from Richmond, also included flat prohibitions. He specified mandatory—

not precatory—protections of such basic rights as freedom of religion, press, and assembly, and followed them with the explicit statement that all "exceptions . . . shall not be construed as to diminish the just importance of other rights retained by the people" and were "inserted merely for greater caution."[40] From this step it was not difficult to place in the Bill of Rights two of the greatest "savings clauses" possible: the Ninth and Tenth Amendments, which remain to this day guarantors of the inherent, residuary rights of the people and the community. Nevertheless, Madison continued to fear state governments no less than a national government as threats to the people's rights. Each sector must continue to operate in tandem as a check on the other; even state "laws are unconstitutional which infringe the rights of the community," and they must be controlled from above.[41]

No sooner had the federal Bill of Rights been debated and sent on to states for ratification than Virginians in Congress set to work accommodating regional needs to national institutions—in fact, they set to work preserving local justice *through* national institutions; that is, they worked to create a federal judiciary that would allow local variation within a "supreme law of the land." It is no accident that Richard Henry Lee, a prominent Virginia Antifederalist, chose to serve on the Senate Judiciary Committee charged with the task of creating a federal court system, and no coincidence that Lee introduced on the Senate floor the first of the federal judicial Process Acts that preserved state jurisprudence by making the first inferior courts into state courts for many purposes. In those acts we see the various legacies of concern and custom, parochial and extensive jurisprudence, that colonial Virginia bequeathed to the commonwealth. So, too, do we see these legacies balanced in the federal Judiciary Act of 1789, which balanced state and local powers in the federal court system. It is entirely appropriate (though entirely unplanned) that at this very minute a United States district court is hearing cases on this campus, just a few hundred yards away at the law school, as part of this intertwined jurisprudence.

The same controversy that dominated Virginia's attempt to balance local and national imperatives within a context of federalism would burst into more agonizing debate throughout Southern history. Virginians, like other Southerners, had to grapple with their own needs and understandings within a national enterprise whose basic fundamental goals they shared. It is important for us to recognize that the twisting and backtracking of Southerners in Antebellum national debate were not merely self-conscious contradictions or expediently convenient shifts to accommodate the unanticipated needs of the moment when the slavery issue wrenched them into constitutional conflict, just as they had not been in 1787. These ambivalences had been present from the earliest days of the nation—indeed, they were older than the idea of a nation. They were a legacy of Virginia's own colonial history, and were a goal as implicitly understood as it was resistant to explicit formulation.

# The "Amending Fathers" and the Constitution: Changing Perceptions of Home Rule and Who Should Rule at Home

EDWARD C. PAPENFUSE, JR.

In the last two decades of the 18th century, the purpose of representative government shifted from minimal services and a means of redressing grievances by petition to the legislature, to an ever-increasing involvement in public expenditure and regulation of the private world. The concept of who was represented changed from men of property to all white men who had a stake in whatever action government took. At the same time the perception of who should govern changed, although not as rapidly. As Richard Hofstadter has pointed out, those in power only reluctantly relinquished the notion that on balance parties were evil and that only those with relatively high stakes (defined as property) should rule. At the outset of the struggle over the Constitution the perception within the elite of what constituted a "good" ruler was probably very close to the obituary of the Virginian Edmund Pendleton as quoted by Hofstadter:

> None of his opinions were drawn from personal views or party prejudices. He never had a connection with any political party . . . so that his opinions were the result of his own judgement, and that judgement was rendered upon the best unbiased estimate he could make of the public good.[1]

Several years after George Washington's death and in the midst of a second war with Great Britain, Thomas Jefferson remembered that Washington "often declared to me that he considered our new Constitution as an experiment on the practicability of republican government, and with what dose of liberty man could be trusted for his own good."[2] The Debate over the adoption and amendment of the Constitution commenced a strenuous test of that experiment that would lead to political consequences far beyond any that Washington, Jefferson, or the majority of their contemporaries could imagine. The struggle over the Constitution, and specifically, a Bill of Rights, transformed a political culture of shifting alliances and small factions centered on forceful personalities into a movement towards "peaceable assemblies" called parties, that sought after leaders who reflected their interests and their concerns.

I

Beginning in 1776, each of the revolting colonies created formal governmental structures at the state level that, for the most part, proved viable even in the light of a remarkable change in the economic demands placed upon the political world. War irrevocably altered the nature of government and the services it was expected to provide.[3] The Treaty of Paris in 1783, ratified while Congress was sitting in Annapolis, thrust the 13 loosely associated former colonies on to the international scene without there being any clear idea of how each of those new States ought to act. At the same time war also changed the popular perception of what government was meant to do. Government grew larger, levied heavy taxes, and became more involved in public services such as education and internal improvements (e.g. in Maryland, the formation of the University of Maryland and the efforts to improve both the Potomac and Susquehanna Rivers). Within the context of the local government created under its first written state constitution, Maryland, like most other states, learned to spend money for "public" reasons on a scale hitherto unknown, and at the expense of a national debt concurrently being created on its behalf. The

American Revolution taught local American Government how to raise money from taxes, and it did not take long to accustom those who governed to enjoy the power and patronage that went with spending it. Through the constitutions they created and the governments that resulted, states like Maryland questioned whether or not they needed to meet obligations—financial or other beyond their state boundaries.[4]

Perceptions of what representative government ought to be also changed from a government of the better sort, the social and economic elite, ruling in the best interest of the governed (as they saw it) to a tendency toward referendum and recall. In 1787, one "Constituent" summarized both the prevailing view of a good legislator and the reality of factional local politics in an article in the *Maryland Gazette and Baltimore Advertiser.* Legislators he wrote, *should be*

> men who can read the human character, and know what will best suit the circumstances, habits and dispositions of the people—men whose minds are enlightened and improved by experience and observation, which ever information on constitutional and legislative deliberations. Those also, and those alone, are deserving of [the voter's] patronage, who can have no motive to oppose the general good, or throw the State into disorder, from party violence, factious combinations, disappointed resentments, or pinching want. Of all such beware, or you will repent of your folly too late to prevent its injurious effects. . . . Property is the ground of distinction between freemen and slaves in our excellent constitution—they who have a certain proportion in consequences of it, possess the right of suffrage, while all who have not, are on that account disqualified.[5]

Within two decades party allegiance would begin to take precedence over personal rectitude, and representatives would be expected to be more responsive than responsible.

It is important not to forget that politics and political theory at the local level has much to do with how and why a national government such as that proposed by the Constitution came to be. The individual states tried first to govern themselves and, for a decade, their experiments in self-government functioned rather well. A few within the local governing elite, however, saw the need to solve some problems beyond state boundaries, by addressing a few issues regionally and even nationally (e.g. the Mount Vernon Compact of April 1785; the Annapolis Convention of September 1786). When these efforts proved successful, some pushed further for a national convocation embracing all 13 new states to:

> take into consideration the situation of the United States; to devise such further provisions as shall appear to them necessary to render the constitution of the federal government adequate to the exigencies of the union; and to report such an act for that purpose to the United States in Congress assembled pursuant to the thirteenth article of the confederation, as when agreed to by them, and afterwards confirmed by the legislatures of every state, will effectually provide for the same.[6]

It is from the local context, however, that the issues of commerce, defense, war debt, and the meaning of the "vox populi" and representative government arose. This does not mean that the national political forum, as provided by Congress, was not important, but until at least 1789, that forum was decidedly secondary to developments on the local level. This is confirmed over and over again by a close examination of the proceedings of Congress. Not even Congressmen took Congress seriously. A good example is the Annapolis experience of the winter and spring of 1783–1784, as described by Thomas Jefferson:

> Congress had now become a very small body, and the members very remiss in their attendance on its duties, insomuch, that a majority of the States, necessary by the Confederation to constitute a House even for minor business, did not assemble until the 13th of December [1783]. . . .
> Our body was little numerous, but very contentious. Day after day was wasted on the most unimportant question. A member, one of those afflicted with the morbid rage of debate, of an ardent mind, prompt imagination, and copious flow of words,

who heard with impatience any logic which was not his own,
sitting near me on some occasion of a trifling but wordy debate,
asked me how I could sit in silence, hearing so much false
reasoning, which a word should refute? I observed to him, that
to refute indeed was easy, but to silence was impossible.[7]

With the publication of the proposed Federal Constitution (for
Maryland that was September 22, 1787) the first nationally focused
political campaign began in earnest.[8] The Federalists were unwilling to modify their creation, but the Anti-Federalists succeeded in
persuading the electorate (albeit a relatively restricted one) that
the new Constitution should contain a Bill of Rights to protect the
individual and each state against arbitrary power. As one correspondent in the local newspaper put it, who was to say how
virtuous our Federal representatives will be in several years.

In Maryland the Federalists proved to be a loose coalition of

a) those within the governing elite (frequently with ties to the
war-time military establishment) who favored a "strong dollar,"
national constitution and assumption of the war debt, a strong
national defense, a united front in foreign affairs, protection of
trade, public encouragement of a nationwide industry and
b) former closet loyalists (nonjurors) who were convinced by
Tench Coxe that the new national constitution was truly better
than the old British one. There were no rotten boroughs, no
"corruption," no "tyrants," and yet "English liberties" were
safeguarded.[9]

Anti-Federalists were a loose coalition of

a) those within the ruling elite who believed small government
was good government,
b) debtors, large and small who, were desperate for debt relief
(as opposed to debtors who could withstand pressure to pay
their debts because of diversified investments and better management of available resources)
c) ideological republicans who favored the independent farmer
and distrusted the growing urban corruption of Baltimore, who
feared arbitrary power in any form, who like the transplanted
Virginian, John Francis Mercer, demanded that those who supported the Revolution risking their lives and fortune be given

special privileges for their wartime sacrifices and insisted that personal liberties be safeguarded along with states' rights in written form.[10]

In the end both achieved a measure of success. The Federalists, building on existing state constitutional experience, provided the structure of the national government. The Anti-Federalists (more appropriately referred to as the "Amending Fathers"), provided the framework of individual protection in the first ten Amendments and laid the groundwork both philosophically and practically for the expansion of the electorate that, in time, led to profound changes and tensions within American politics.

In attempting to assess local political issues as they affected the course of national politics, great care must be taken, not to exaggerate their long-term importance. For example, there is no question that the success of Daniel Shays' rebellion in Massachusetts in 1786, did temporarily raise the anxiety level of the existing political leadership in Maryland as elsewhere, but as Uriah Forrest, a member of the House of Delegates, observed to Thomas Jefferson, then in Paris, "the most trifling events have been magnified into monstrous outrages." Would, he wondered, the next generation "credit us, that in the first twelve years of the independence of thirteen free powerful and separate states, only one rebellion happened." Jefferson's well-known response that "a little rebellion" was a "good thing," has helped to obscure the fact that by the time the debate over the adoption of the Constitution was begun in earnest, Shays' Rebellion had been controlled locally and was largely ignored nationally.[11]

In 1788 as in 1776, political memories were relatively short and poorly focused. Politics at the local level were episodic, factious, deference-oriented, and left little room for any persistent theme of "party" or party organization focusing on long-term objectives of obtaining or holding political power.[12] Perhaps the most perceptive analysis of contemporary factious politics, politics that were devoid of any sense of party politics as understood today, was written by James Madison in *Federalist #10*, first published in

November 1787. Ironically it was this and the other Federalist polemics that were to be instrumental in providing the theoretical nucleus for the development of an essentially two-party structure for the future of American politics, but in 1787 the local political climate was quite different. Madison's defense of how government should work remains problematic, but no one has more skillfully or accurately portrayed the reality of the Maryland, and possibly all, local political systems than Madison. Those were systems in which a kaleidoscopic array of interests working within the framework of a very limited constituency, struggle to control the sources of power. Indeed it was a struggle for political power that was increasingly viewed with *envy* by those excluded from it, and with *fear* by that "prevailing and increasing distrust of public engagements, and claim for private rights, which are echoed from one of the continent to the other." The process of state constitution-writing that began in 1776, and to which Madison refers in the *Federalist #10*, institutionalized factional politics at the local level. At the same time it provided the framework for a national Constitution in which one day party would be institutionalized and would lead to a fundamental alteration in the definition of the "vox populi" in American Politics.[13]

## II

In May 1776, on eve of what Samuel Chase referred to as the "Decisive Blow" for Independence, Thomas Stone (with Chase, a signer of the Declaration of Independence) would write a long and thoughtful letter to the political leadership of Maryland suggesting the need to pay heed to the voice of the people:

> The Vox Populi must in great measure influence your determination of the part to be taken by the Province [of Maryland with regard to the issue of Independence] . . . You must . . . declare explicitly that you will go all Lengths with the majority of Congress or that you will not join in a War to be carried on for the purposes of Independency & new establishments, and will

break the Union, . . . either of which are dangerous extremes—
But whatever is determined it will be wise and prudent to have
the concurrence of the People.[14]

What Stone meant by the "concurrence of the people," of
course, is critical to an understanding of the course of American
political development. In 1776 it meant one thing. After 1787, it
began to mean something quite different.

In 1776 there was considerable ambivalence about the role the
electorate should play in government, although throughout the
colonies there was universal desire to write down on paper in a
Constitution just how state governments should be organized and
to explain in some detail what that government could and could not
do. With few exceptions, beginning in 1776 all the state conventions began by drafting a "Declaration" or "Bill" of Rights. Virginia
was first, and with the help of George Mason's inspired pen,
produced a model containing sixteen articles for the other states to
follow. Maryland obliged later that same fall with a declaration of
rights almost three times as long as Virginia's, and the longest any
state would attempt.[15]

In Maryland the movement for a written declaration of rights
(and responsibilities) of the people began in earnest in the weeks
preceding the call for a Constitutional Convention. On the day that
Virginia adopted its Constitution (June 27, 1776), a small band of
discontented citizens of Anne Arundel County issued a twenty-
two point manifesto calling for a new "Form of Government" in
which

> The right to legislate is in every member of the community: . . .
> for the sake of convenience the excercise of such right must be
> delegated to certain persons, to be chosen by the people:
> "When this choice is free, it is the peoples['] fault if they are not
> happy . . .
> It is essential to liberty, [argued the Anne Arundel Committee],
> that the legislative, judicial and executive powers of government
> be separate from the each; for where they are united in the same
> person or a number of persons there would be wanting that
> mutual check which is the principal security against . . . arbi-

trary laws, and a wanton excercise of power in the execution of them.[16]

Some of those already in power, such as Charles Carroll of Carrollton, were uncomfortable with the Anne Arundel Committee and the concerns it raised. Carroll called their leaders levelers and spoke disparagingly of them as emanating from a democratic element. Yet the Convention that met in August 1776 adopted the majority of their proposals and much of their language into a Declaration of Rights and Form of Government that was implemented without dissent in February, 1776, after having submitted a complete draft to the electorate for their consideration.[17]

On September 17, 1776, eleven years to the day before the United States Constitution was signed in Philadelphia, the convention which produced the first written constitution for the state of Maryland adopted a motion that took the proposed declaration of rights and state constitution to the people several weeks *before* its final passage on November 8, 1776. The words of the motion adopted by the Maryland Convention on September 17, 1776 are particularly significant in light of what happened eleven years later when the National Convention in Philadelphia refused to consider any "Bill" or "Declaration" of Rights. The resolution of September 17, 1776 reads:

> the establishing of bill of rights and the formation of a new government on the authority of the people only, are matters of the utmost importance to the good people of this state and their posterity.

If further resolved that

> the said bill of rights and form of government be immediately printed for the consideration of the people at large, and that twelve copies thereof be sent without delay to each county of this state.[18]

### The Right of the People Peaceably to Assemble

The various State Constitution both as written after 1776 and what was derived from practice in the intervening years made constitution writing in the summer of 1787 for a national government a relatively simple, if not painless, task. Yet the convention which met in Philadelphia in the summer of 1787, misjudged the reaction of its intended audience which the First Congress under the new Constitution moved quickly to rectify. It failed to realize that there would be a widespread demand for some written form of "Declaration" or "Bill" of "Rights." Like Maryland, in 1787 almost all state constitutions had a bill of rights or declaration of rights either embodied in their text or as separate documents. When none was added to the proposed Federal Constitution, it did not take long before the critics of the Constitution began to ask why.

### III

In examining the debate over the adoption of the Constitution and its amendment by a bill of rights it is important to distinguish between unqualified opposition to any constitution and the efforts to further define the rights and privileges encompassed by the product of the Philadelphia Convention. Within Maryland and probably elsewhere most of the concern over the Constitution centered on the lack of a bill of rights and not over the question of the need for "a more perfect union." Indeed that 12 percent or so of the population who had a choice in the matter were generally apathetic and were content to accept the recommendations of the Philadelphia Convention.[19] This does not mean that they would not also support amendments if they were proposed and their purpose explained.

Initially the explanations of those unhappy with the Constitution proved ill-defined and poorly articulated. In Pennsylvania and Massachusetts vocal minorities protested that a declaration or bill of rights was needed, but until a ratification convention was called for in Maryland there was nothing like a substantive agenda for the electorate to react to and to act upon. Even then the "Amending Fathers" were slow to coordinate their efforts and to launch an effective campaign. For example, when "two gentlemen" of Washington County tried "to stir up the minds of the common people against the new constitution" a meeting was called in Hagerstown to discuss in detail the provisions of the document. That meeting in turn called for another to counter the "scurrilous language" about the Constitution then appearing in the *Carlisle [Pennsylvania] Gazette* which one irate reader argued was "calculated to inflame and irritate the minds of the contending parties, and run them to desperation, instead of harmony and amenity." The second meeting was held on March 1, a month and a half before the Maryland Ratifying Convention was to meet in Annapolis. It proved even more supportive of the Constitution than the first. As reported in the *Carlisle Gazette,*

> the people of this county (considering the shortness of the time) had a pretty general notice of the meeting, and accordingly assembled, at the court house, to a very considerable number." At one the doors were open. Elijah Gaither was appointed to read and explain the Constitution in English, while Abraham Faw, a member of the House of Delegates from Frederick County, did likewise in German. These gentlemen very coolly and ably read and explained the plan, section by section, and clause by clause, to the general satisfaction of all present, the chairman at intervals calling on the populace, if any among them had objections to any of the articles, sections, clauses, or provisions, to state them, in order that they might be answered, and the doubts cleared up, but contrary to my expectations, (knowing that some of the gentlemen were in the assembly, that heretofore had made such extraordinary exertions to prejudice the minds of the common people against the plan, by misrepresentations:) not one objection was offered, or a dissenting voice heard . . .

By early 1788, most of the concrete concerns about the Constitution that had been aired in writing were confined to the minorities of Pennsylvania and Massachusetts and did not seem to convince the crowd. The *Gazette's* correspondent did concede that the Federalists (among whom he counted himself) had been so zealous in their criticism of the Constitution's detractors that some were reluctant to speak out. He chastised his friends and closed with the hope that

> after some short time, we will be unanimous in our opinions, and as soon as nine states shall ratify, (which I have no doubt but such ratification will take place before the first of July next, as it is allowed, there will be little or no opposition in the convention of this state) I hope we will be all unanimous in rejoicing on the joyful event, and burying all discord and animosity in oblivion, with the old articles of confederation.[20]

In part his hope was justified. Maryland did ratify the Constitution without amendment, but the small minority of delegates who favored amendment had an influence on the future course of events far greater than their numbers might indicate.

In Maryland the Amending Fathers finally developed a convincing platform for a Federal Bill of Rights in early April 1788, even if it came too late to change the minds of the electorate in more than a handful of counties prior to the Maryland ratifying convention. The proposals of the minority at the Maryland Convention (April 21–28, 1788) as widely distributed in the newspapers and in a pamphlet printed that summer in Richmond, touched a responsive chord throughout the nation, but especially in those states that had not yet ratified. Maryland was the catalyst and William Paca, who had served on the committee that drafted Maryland's Declaration of Rights in 1776, was the principal instigator, drawing his inspiration from the document he and six others had written eleven years before.

In a special issue of the *Maryland Historical Magazine*, Dr. Gregory Stiverson has ably documented the work of the minority at the Maryland Ratifying Convention.[21] There were twelve men who pledged themselves to the amendment of the Constitution. They were led by William Paca, Samuel Chase, and Luther Martin. They represented three counties, Harford, Baltimore, and Anne Arundel, all of which were within one good day's riding by horseback from their existing bases of local political support. They were men of principle who proved to be more representative of the sentiments of the people generally than did the majority in either Philadelphia or Annapolis. Indeed, to join his friend William Paca, Samuel Chase sacrificed his political career in Baltimore City.

William Paca offered twenty-two amendments to the Maryland Convention, over half of which were taken verbatim from the 1776 Declaration of Rights. At first it seemed as if the minority might be able to convince the majority of Convention delegates to entertain amendments, but the sentiments for unqualified ratification proved too strong. Paca joined the majority explaining that:

> As to the line of conduct which I shall now pursue, I thus publicly declare, that exceptionable as this government is, and liable to all these objections . . . I hope and trust, that its defects may be hereafter corrected.

After the decisive vote was taken (63 to 11 in favor of unqualified ratification), Paca then

> laid upon the table a list of amendments, which [the *Pennsylvania Packet* reported] will be considered by the gentlemen, and those that approved of by them, in the capacity as citizens, not as members of convention, will be recommended by them to the legislature, who may, if they think proper, instruct the delegates to the first Federal Congress to press their adoption.[22]

In the end it was the report of the minority as it appeared in the May 6, 1788 *Maryland Gazette and Baltimore Advertiser* and as a broadside, that proved the critical agenda for reform. It gave the nearly evenly divided Virginia Convention a detailed list of amendments to discuss and debate in the context of the Declaration of Rights imbedded within their own state constitution. As Dr. Stiverson points out, at least a quarter of the amendments proposed by the Virginia ratifying convention were drawn from the Maryland context. Indeed third on Virginia's list was a provision based upon the fourth article of the 1776 Maryland Declaration of Rights, a provision that was unique among the state constitutions and with minor modification headed the list of amendments first proposed by William Paca to the Maryland convention:

That it be declared that all persons intrusted with the Legislative or Executive Powers of Government are the Trustees and Servants of the public, and as such accountable for their conduct. Wherefore whenever the ends of Government are perverted and public Liberty manifestly endangered and all other means of Redress are ineffectual, the people may, and of right ought . . . to reform the old or establish a new Government, the doctrine of non Resistance against arbitrary power and Oppression is absurd, slavish and destructive of the Good and Happiness of Mankind.[23]

In any government, determining who should share power and how it should be shared is fundamental to its survival. In 1776 the balancing of Legislative, Executive, and Judicial power at the local level was begun in earnest with the writing of the state constitutions. At issue was not only the structure and form of government, but also the definition of who should choose those who govern.

In asserting that there was universal support for some form of written declaration of rights within the American political constituency in 1788, care must be taken to not confuse those few Anti-Federalists who opposed *Big,* powerful, and expensive central government (such as the Charles Ridgelys in Maryland) with the vast majority of enfranchised Americans (mostly propertied men) who clearly favored a carefully written statement of "Rights" to be retained by individuals and the states under the new Constitution.

In looking at how the Constitution came to be adopted and amended it is also important to keep in mind that there are 13 constitutions (14, counting Vermont), and that there were 13 or 14 "Polities"—political environments from which emerged a national consensus on how the national government should be structured and constrained. No one locality could lay claim to more than suggesting ideas that others might modify. It is possible to assert with some degree of certainty, however, that the collective effort of developing the language for the First Amendment created a concept fundamental to the legitimization of political parties and political action. Furthermore, the Maryland contribution to its wording and ultimate adoption marked a significant shift in attitudes towards political behavior, particularly in the context of those 'peaceable assemblies' that became political parties.

Perhaps the best single secondary source on the historical origins of the first amendments to the Constitution is Judge Edward Dumbauld's "State Precedents for the Bill of Rights."[24] Dumbauld makes it abundantly clear that James Madison played the major role in articulating the concerns over the Constitution as presented for ratification to the states, and that he was instrumental in seeing the first amendments through the First Congress. Madison worked from a printed compilation of amendments, proposed by New York, Massachusetts, New Hampshire, Maryland, and South Carolina which he sent to Jefferson in October of 1788. Dumbauld argues convincingly that the sequencing of the New York amendments was adopted by Madison as a way of incorporating them directly into the *Body* of the Constitution. In this way Madison hoped to ignore any of the Constitution, while the others became part of the language of the document itself. To that extent he failed. The pressure to have a separate statement of individual freedoms and states' rights was simply too great.

But while James Madison applied his indisputable genius to the final form of the Bill of Rights, the language and intent of those ratified amendments had its origins in the conventions called at the local level between 1776 and 1788. Take for example the evolution of the language of the First Amendment which in final form reads:

> Congress shall make no law respecting an establishment of religion, or prohibiting the free exercise thereof; or abridging the freedom of speech, or of the press, or the right of the people peaceably to assemble and to petition the Government for a redress or grievances.

The final text of the First Amendment [1791] contains five separate and distinct elements:

1) Freedom of Religion
2) Freedom of Speech
3) Freedom of the Press
4) Freedom to Peaceably Assemble
5) Freedom to Petition the Government for Redress of Grievances

They, in part, derive from the Virginia Declaration of Rights [6/1776] (in Paragraph 16 and 12) which addresses:

1) Religion
3) Press

but NOT:

2) Speech
4) Peaceable Assembly or
5) Petition for Redress of Grievances

The Maryland Declaration of Rights [11/1776] (in Sections 11, 33, 35, 38) expands the rights enumerated by Virginia to include:

4) Freedom to Petition and
2) Speech as far as assembly goes, but *not* expressly Freedom to *Peaceably assemble* or to petition for Redress or Grievances.

It was not until the draft United States Constitution was dispatched to the states by Congress in September 1787, that the Fifth proposition of the First Amendment was delineated. On September 27, 1787, Congressman Richard Henry Lee proposed an amendment "that the right of the people to assemble peaceably for the purpose of petitioning the legislature shall not be prevented," but it too lacked any reference to peaceably assembly for any other purposes than to *petition* the legislature.[25]

William Paca's Amendments to the Federal Constitution presented to the Maryland Ratifying Convention in April 1788, and as printed in the pamphlet and broadside used by Madison in formulating his draft of the Bill of Rights, encompassed

1) Religion
2) Speech
3) Press and
4) Petition (as an individual),

but do not clearly mention collective action in peaceable assembly except to the extent that "every man has both a right to petition the Legislature, for the Redress of Grievances, in a peaceable and orderly manner." [26] It was left to Virginia two months later to add, as a result of a ratifying convention marked by close division and sharp controversy:

> that the people have a right peaceably to assemble together to consult for the common good, or to instruct their representatives, and that every human has a right to petition or apply to the legislature. [27]

If the premise is accepted that political parties derive their basic right to organize, petition, assemble, etc. from the protection of the First Amendment, then the theory behind such protection to which all the states ultimately subscribed was derived in spirit and language from local Maryland and Virginia politics beginning as early as 1776. By 1791 the 'Vox Populi' to which Thomas Stone referred in 1776 had undergone a significant transformation in meaning from recourse to a largely passive and ambiguous ill-defined ideal to any number of people possessing the legally specified right of "peaceable assembly."

## IV

In the 1780s at most 11.12% of the total population and 16.41% of the white population were permitted to vote under terms of a Maryland Constitution which limited the franchise to:

> all freemen of 21, free holding of 50 acres and all freemen having 30 pounds of personal property (about 66% of the free white males over 21). [28]

Even in the most contested of the elections for members to Maryland's ratifying convention, only about 42% of those eligible voted. In Baltimore Town, for example, 1,338 people (white adult males) of about 3,208 eligible in a city of 19,557 free citizens) elected James McHenry to the Ratifying Convention in January of

1788. At the same time in Washington County (with a white population of 14,536) at most, 29% of the eligible voters showed up to send their representatives to the Annapolis Ratifying Convention.[29] In short, voter turnout was even lower 200 years ago than it is today.

Some scholars might attribute this lack of concern and voter apathy to a pervasive desire not to be involved in the public world. Perhaps, but what it does provide is a quite different setting for politics as usual than we know or understand today. The thesis proposed here is that in Maryland the political elite or oligarchy was well integrated into the economic elite by 1776 and continued to keep control over political affairs until the last decade of the century.[30] From this perspective, the controversy over paper money and debtor/creditor relationships coupled with speculation and greed (the Black list; Samuel Chase and the attempt to corner the grain market in 1778), are largely squabbles within the elite. Furthermore they were conflicts within a highly fragmented and factious political arena about which few people in general really cared, beyond tavern gossip and generally accepted norms of what constituted good, but not very consequential, entertainment. After all the furor over Samuel Chase's move to Baltimore in September of 1787, and the scurrilous newspaper attacks by him and about him in the newspapers, the report of the election in the paper the next day placed it all in perspective:

> A correspondent observes that by a great number of publications in the papers, and hand-bills, the attention of the public has been endeavoured to be drawn to the election of delegates for this town; and to warm and great opposition that was announced to be made to the election of Samuel Chase, Esq who offered to represent this town in the General Assembly. On Wednesday last [October 3], at noon the polls were closed and, of 830 votes, the numbers for the candidates were as follows.—Samuel Chase, 612 . . .[31]

This is not to suggest that no issues transcended the in-house bickering of a politically secure elite. At times economic or political crises like war and a shortage of coin could. But it took the intensive debate over the adoption and amendment of the Constitution before there emerged any concerted effort to redefine the electorate and its relationship to its representatives. In the decade after 1776, much as in the several generations before, the political world was still confined to a relatively small number of families who could speak with confidence for the people who stood viva voce to elect them. [32]

The pressures from the military in 1776 (not unlike the demands of Cromwell's army in the 1640s), to expand participation in the political process to all who bore arms was a temporary and controllable phenomenon, brought about by the exigencies of war, and led by Rezin Hammond, a well-established member of the planter elite. [33] But the effort to define the political constituency by other members of the elite such as John Francis Mercer was a long-term pressure of a different sort brought about by the exigencies of a peace in which the old methods of maintaining the planter/merchant hegemony were increasingly subject to question.

The American Revolution made government into potentially a large, profitable business and converted the arena of local (meaning state) government from a factious debating club with few actions of long term consequences, into a source of extensive, and tempting, economic power. The process of constitution making that culminated in the adoption and amendment of the Federal Constitution, legitimized "peaceable assemblies," soon to be known as political parties. Parties in turn proved an excellent vehicle for further expanding the franchise to all free white adult males in 1802. In the 1780s, however, the developments of the next two decades were still largely figments of the fearful imagination of such social and political conservatives as Charles Carroll of Carrollton. [34] Those in the state among the political elite who found they were constantly excluded from the control of government after 1776, sought first to enlarge their support within the existing electorate, following well-established rules of behavior.

Samuel Chase, a clear loser in the paper money issues of

1785/1786, moved to Baltimore in 1787 where he assumed that he could continue to participate in the political process on the strength of his position in the elite, and his many years of service in Legislature. In his first election in Baltimore City, Chase's assessment proved correct, coming only a few days after the publication of the final draft of the proposed United States Constitution in the Baltimore newspapers. There was not yet an opportunity for the debate over the proposed Constitution to impinge upon the question of who would best represent Baltimore City's interests in the legislature. Chase won handily over James McHenry. But by April 1788 politics at the national and local level had changed dramatically. The debate over the constitution had irrevocably altered attitudes in the City of Baltimore, if not the countryside, toward the nature of representation and what a representative ought to be.[35]

In the controversy over paper money Chase had advocated a return "to the people" for instructions, secure in the knowledge that his view of what ought to be done coincided with what the "people" wanted: cheap paper money and a lenient debt policy. In effect, he looked to the referendum on paper money as a confirmation of a position he had already assumed based upon his role as a "Virtuous" and "Virtual" representative of the people, who having chosen him, then left him free to act on his good judgement. In 1787 Chase assumed that his good judgement on the constitution, which was to defeat or at least amend it, would prevail with his constituents in Baltimore City. It did not, and he was soundly defeated, first at the elections in April for the ratifying convention, and then the following fall when McHenry reversed the vote of a year before.[36]

The election of October 1788 for delegates to the Maryland General Assembly was a turning point in Maryland, and quite probably, national political history. Simply put, the election of 1788 was the first election in which national issues played a critical role in shaping the organization of local politics in a permanent manner. It was in the interest of Baltimore City to support the Constitution be cause of what it promised for the economic protection of the city and of its future development as a port and a manufacturing center.[37]

The rest of Maryland supported the Constitution too, but for entirely different reasons. They, in contrast to the constituency of Baltimore City who "led" their representatives to support the Constitution, deferred to their representatives in the old tradition of Maryland politics. Nothing demonstrates this rule of behavior better than the success Chase and Mercer had in the countryside as they tried to rally opposition to ratification of the new Constitution. Chase and Mercer found that they could work within the old system in the county side to sway the existing constituency to their point of view. Witness their triumphs in Anne Arundel, Baltimore and Harford Counties in April 1788.

While Samuel Chase, who had abandoned his Baltimore City constituents to the Federalists, went into one part of Anne Arundel County and harangued the electorate, John Francis Mercer and Jeremiah Chase went into another where they dispersed a signed hand bill summarizing their "platform":

Bill of Rights
Liberty of Conscience.
Trial by Jury.
No Excise
No Poll Tax.
No Standing Army in Peace,
Without Limitation.
No Whipping Militia,
Nor Marching Them Out Of
The State, Without Consent
Of The General Assembly.
No Direct Taxation,
Without Previous Requisition.

According to Daniel Carroll, the result was that "the people were alarmed at their positive assertions, and I am assured when they attended the Polls, a wilderness appeared in many which show'd they were really frightened by what they had just heard." Undoubtedly similar campaigns were waged by William Paca in Harford County and Captain Charles Ridgely in Baltimore County, where pro-amendment candidates were elected. Nevertheless, slates favoring unqualified ratification prevailed elsewhere in Maryland. Probably the major reason why the pro-amendment forces had such limited success in the countryside was their tardiness. Four days was not enough time to canvass effectively and distribute handbills beyond an area within a day or two's riding of Baltimore City. It may also be that Samuel Chase took too long to make up his mind to join with William Paca in a concerted attack on those who supported unqualified ratification, thus preventing any organized effort until it was too late.[38]

Those who controlled the reins of power had not been idle either, although neither they nor their opponents in the legislature probably realized the political implications of their action. By January of 1787 a bill was passed by the legislature that welcomed back into the fold all that silent third of the population that had never been enamored with the Revolution in the first place. These were the non-jurors, the silent Tories, who refused to participate in the political process after 1776 because of the "Oath of Allegiance" written into the Constitution, but did not join the Loyalist migration. They were men like William Tilghman, brother of Washington's aide Tench Tilghman, and Harry Dorsey Gough, relative and political foe of Charles Ridgely. As William Tilghman explained to Tench Coxe in February 1787:

> I should tell you that before our Assembly rose, they gave the most ample and liberal relief to the whole body of Nonjurors— Upon taking an unexceptionable Oath of Allegiance, they are entitled to all priveledges of citizenship—The legal barriers now removed, I imagine, I ought without much difficulty take a part in public affairs.[39]

In 1788 Tilghman returned to the House of Delegates along with Henry Dorsey Gough, in time for Tilghman to take up the cause of the ratification of the Bill of Rights as proposed by the First U.S. Congress.[40] By January 21, 1790, the *Charleston* [*South Carolina*]

*Morning Post & City Register* could report that the Maryland Legislature

> unanimously adopted the amendments to the Federal Constitution recommended by the Senate and House of Representatives of the United States. In one of the articles it is said, "That congress shall make no laws abridging the freedom of speech or of the press." If the supreme legislature of the union, can make no laws on the subject, the press is free indeed! and the state legislatures cannot interfere therein, much less can any of the county courts pretend to set bounds to that which, by the wise and constitutional declaration of a free people, is not under the control of their superiors. [41]

It would, perhaps, not be too much of an exaggeration to observe, that with the changes in requirements for taking the oath of allegiance at the local level, and with the adoption of the National Constitution, the closet loyalists, the non jurors, were likely candidates for admission to the ranks of a nationalist, or "Federalist," party. At the same time, those of the Maryland elite, such as John Francis Mercer, who had struggled to prevent declared loyalists from voting, and had supported the claims of those who had paid their pre-war debts in depreciated currency (those of "Black list" fame), now adopted the cause of expanding the franchise to encompass men who had never before participated in the political process, in order to gain control of Maryland government. [42]

Samuel Chase did not find the "new" politics to his liking. He clearly preferred the old electoral system and quickly retreated into the arms of the Federalist Party in a successful search for a Federal judicial sinecure. John Francis Mercer, on the other hand, in the countryside, and the likes of Samuel Smith in the city, persisted until they achieved universal white manhood suffrage and the paper ballot. In doing so, they fundamentally altered the course of American politics in a way that neither probably ever intended. Near the end of his life Mercer would write a pamphlet decrying the efforts to make the sinful city of Baltimore the State Capital. In doing so he repeated with grateful acknowledgement the arguments of the arch-Federalist Alexander Contee Hanson that too much democracy could proved fatal to good government.[43]

The years from the fall of 1787 to 1802 were years of transformation of the political system in Maryland at the local level. Until 1787, politics in Maryland functioned like it had for two or more previous generations. That is not to say that some within the governing elite did not worry. Professor Ronald Hoffman has amply documented the levels of concern during the worst of the war years.[44] But those concerns were ameliorated by peace and played little part in the controversies of the late 1780s. It was not until *National* issues such as the regulation of trade and the posture of the thirteen colonies in the world, could no longer be ignored, that changes in the definitions of "vox populi," and in the nature of representative government began to occur.

First with the Annapolis Convention of 1786, and then with the Philadelphia Convention of 1787, the questions of what the character of the National Government should be and how it should affect both local government and individual rights, became issues that forced those in power at the local level to reevaluate their positions and to advocate, in varying degrees and in quite different ways, the expansion of the electorate.

For Maryland at least, the adoption of the Constitution seems to have presented an unprecedented challenge to the longstanding, peaceful hegemony of the governing elite as well as to their basic philosophy of the relationship of citizens to their government. For the first time in a significant and comprehensive way an effort was made to define in writing the "vox populi" in a manner that profoundly affected the future course of American political development.

Who the people are and how they ought to be consulted is the crux of the American experiment with democracy. To date it has survived over two hundred years of sometimes violent debate. In large measure we owe that survival to the persistence of a small minority of dissenters. Two hundred years ago they insisted on

arguing peaceably and in ultimately convincing detail for amendments that better defined the rights and responsibilities of the
governed while reserving the privilege of further definition for
future generations. To the Amending Fathers should go the credit
for demonstrating that the "dose of liberty" with which "man could
be trusted for his own good," was limited only by apathy and
ignorance.

# Oral and Written Cultures: North Carolina and the Constitution, 1787–1791

WALTER F. PRATT, JR.

Of all southern states, North Carolina had the least apparent impact on the formation of the Constitution and of the Bill of Rights. The state's delegates to the Constitutional Convention played at best a supporting, editorial role in Philadelphia during the summer of 1787.[1] The state's ratification convention insured that the state would have no voice in the congressional debate on the Bill of Rights by refusing to approve the Constitution until amendments had been proposed.[2] Then, once Congress proposed amendments, North Carolina ratified the Constitution and approved the Bill of Rights in quick succession and with little controversy[3]—accepting the Bill of Rights even before it knew of the decision of any other state.[4]

Yet, in many ways North Carolina's hesitant attitude toward the Constitution is more representative of the attitude of the country than is the overwhelming approval in the other southern states, save Virginia.[5] Even though North Carolina's Antifederalist majority lacked a spokesman with national prominence, the state's skepticism captured well the spirit of the Antifederalist critique of the Constitution. In particular, the debate in North Carolina epitomized the apprehensions provoked by a key characteristic of the proposed Constitution—a characteristic so obvious that it is seldom commented upon. That characteristic is the fact that the Constitution is *written*.[6]

Therefore, in discussing North Carolina's treatment of the Constitution, I want to take seriously that distinctive characteristic of the document. For North Carolina, and much of the rest of the nation, this written, national constitution was a culminating part of an evolution from an oral culture to a written one. That is not to suggest an abrupt change in the final quarter of the eighteenth century. Much of the nation was literate, even if only in having the ability to sign one's name.[7] While oral and written cultures coexisted, though, the important legal and constitutional sub-culture was making the transition from oral to written.[8]

To be sure, the earlier state constitutions (North Carolina's among them) were written, as was the Articles of Confederation. But they did little more than record the practices that had developed either in the individual colonies or through the informal practices of the Continental Congresses.[9] In no case did those documents challenge the localistic communities of the oral tradition. Indeed, the success of the Articles in preserving a state-oriented government was the single most important factor that led to the convention in Philadelphia.[10] Accordingly, none of these documents, though written, posed a significant threat to the communities in which even important, governmental communication continued to be conducted with the participants face-to-face. Virtually everyone, however, recognized that the Constitution was different. It broke with the oral, localistic tradition in that its role was not to preserve but to create a new government.[11] Its supporters sought to impose a national government over the state governments. To do so required a text suited for the purpose, a *written* text with implicit rules for interpretations.[12] The ensuing debate about the Constitution revealed that the Federalists had a sense of hermeneutics; the Antifederalists did not.[13] That difference proved to be especially critical in North Carolina.

Two groups of characteristics distinguish the oral culture from the written.[14] The first of the characteristics describes the communication itself; the second describes the mode of thought that is a consequence of that communication. First, in an oral culture the primary sense for communication is hearing and the primary means for storing information is the human memory. As a consequence, in oral cultures discourse occurs with the speakers face-to-face; meaning, therefore, is highly dependent upon the context. Furthermore, discourse requires special structures to enable the speaker to remember and to enable the audience to understand through hearing.[15] Communication is therefore filled with lists, repetition, and other mnemonic devices to help the speaker (as well as the audience) recall the important points.

Second, in oral culture there are no texts to memorialize knowledge as having an objective existence outside the human mind or independent of context. Thus, oral cultures must devote considerable energy to remembering.[16] The result is a society that tends to be conservative or traditionalist. Finally, because of the necessary interaction between the speaker and the audience, in an oral culture, knowledge must be conceptualized and verbalized in terms of human experience—thought and communication remain closely tied to the human lifeworld.[17]

In a written culture, by contrast, the primary sense for communication is sight, which is removed from the personal context of face-to-face dealings.[18] In the written text, knowledge and communication take on an objective existence apart from human experience. Relieved of the burden of having to devote the mind to remembering, the members of a written culture can begin abstracting principles and analyzing the meaning of writing.

I

North Carolina's rich and discordant colonial history produced a state that falls readily into no single category established for the Constitutional Convention. Statistically North Carolina had become a large state; but intellectually it had little of the cosmopolitan outlook that would drive the large states at the Convention. Excluding what would become Tennessee, North Carolina ranked third in area, behind Virginia and Georgia. In population the Convention ranked it as seventh; though the census of 1790 would show that the state ranked fourth, behind Virginia, Massachusetts, and Pennsylvania.[19]

In spite of the state's size and population, its geography had prevented it from developing into a significant trading state.[20] The outer banks along the Atlantic coast impeded large-scale settlement or trade from the ocean.[21] Once ashore, settlers encountered rivers that did little to facilitate westward transportation. The rivers flowed from the north, closer to Virginia than to western North Carolina; they ended along poorly navigable sections of North Carolina's shore or in South Carolina.[22] North Carolina thus found its trade benefitting the coffers of neighboring Virginia and South Carolina, a fact which prompted James Madison's apt description of North Carolina at the time of the Convention as "a patient bleeding at both arms."[23]

The state's geography also had an impact on the patterns of settlement. The English, who arrived first, dominated the coastal settlements, though the Scots settled in the south-central part of the state. The backcountry was settled much later and then primarily by the Scotch-Irish and Germans.[24] These different national origins accentuated the divergence between east and west, which had begun with difficulties of transportation.

Without substantial commerce and with divergent patterns of settlement, North Carolina was, at the end of the colonial period "virtually all backcountry."[25] As a state without a strong commercial focus or core,[26] it lacked both the commercial and the intellectual ties with the rest of the nation that could provide impetus for a stronger national government.[27] As Hugh Williamson wrote to Governor Alexander Martin (both of whom would later be delegates to the Constitutional Convention) in March 1784, "the Citizens of our State have little foreign commerce, have little intercourse with Strangers and have not so many opportunities of receiving information . . . concerning national & foreign occurrences as are presented to people in large commercial Cities."[28]

Intellectually, the state lacked both the educational and the printing resources necessary to foster links with others outside the state. Public schooling was virtually nonexistent throughout the colonial period.[29] The first teacher on record did not reach the colony until 1706, more than four decades after the first permanent English settlement in the colony.[30] Throughout the remainder of the colonial period, education was sporadic at best, with the limited exceptions provided by tutors in the homes of the well-to-do and by religious groups such as the Moravians. Residents and visitors alike provided similar descriptions of the poor condition of education in the state at the time of the Revolution. Francois Martin, a printer resident in New Bern, wrote that "[l]iterature was hardly known. There were in the whole province but two schools."[31] Likewise, travellers such as Elkanah Watson and John Smyth wrote disparagingly of education in the state. Watson suggested that "[p]erhaps no State had at that period performed so little to promote the cause of education, science and arts, as North Carolina. The lower classes of that region were then in a condition of great mental degradation."[32] Smyth said simply that the residents around Hillsborough (in what was then considered the western part of the state) were "of the very lowest and most ignorant class."[33]

Although there is no way to be certain, it seems that at most a third of the state's population could read.[34] Wills and other records show that there were private collections of books, owned by elite professionals or for the clergy.[35] Even if one were inclined to extrapolate from that limited evidence toward accepting estimates of higher rates of literacy in other colonies,[36] the fact remains that eighteenth-century North Carolina lacked the ability to circulate printed material. The lack of regular post roads before 1770 made it difficult to obtain letters or newspapers from other colonies. Even after 1770, the service was inadequate for at least two decades.[37] Within the colony there were few facilities to compensate for those difficulties with communications. The state had no printing press before 1749.[38] The first newspaper did not appear until 1751.[39] It tried to fill the gap in knowledge by concentrating upon reprinting reports from other colonies and countries.[40] Most people, therefore, had to continue to rely upon word of mouth for local news, thereby reinforcing the existing oral culture. Another significant effect of the limited literacy was lower (because of fewer schools) and opportunities for reading were less (because the few presses were in the east and travel to the west was difficult).[41]

The isolation of the west exacerbated the sectional tensions in state politics. The Regulator uprising of 1771 was the most extreme example of that tension; but the split between east and west antedated the Regulators and continued after the Revolution.[42] That split also stalled efforts to draft a constitution for the state in 1776, during the Fourth Provincial Congress. The regional split forced that congress to leave drafting the constitution to the next congress, which met later the same year.[43] Because no record survives of the debates in that later congress, we cannot know the extent to which there was division over particular provisions. The final document, though, is characteristic of efforts to translate an oral culture into written form.

Most notable about the North Carolina constitution of 1776 is the Declaration of Rights, which precedes the constitution, having been passed the day before the constitution itself. Fletcher Green has made the suggestive observation that "[i]t seems from this procedure that the convention looked upon the Bill [sic] of Rights as more fundamental than the constitution."[44] The North Carolina legislators seemed to be emphasizing, both in time and in text, that the rights of the people were antecedent to the powers of government. Moreover, by using the phrase "*Declaration* of Rights," the drafters recalled the oral tradition of the society in which those rights had grown. The list of twenty-five "rights" is reminiscent of the series of "begats" used in Biblical genealogy or, as Eric Havelock has explicated, the instructions for launching a boat in Homer's *Iliad.*[45] In all three instances, the list serves to enable recollection rather than analysis. For example, the first two provisions seem to be little more than redundancies, until one recognizes their mnemonic function:

I. That all political power is vested in and derived from the people only.

II. That the people of this State ought to have the sole and exclusive right of regulating the internal government and police thereof.[46]

Furthermore, the document itself declares the value of repetition: "a frequent recurrence to fundamental principles is absolutely necessary, to preserve the blessings of liberty."[47]

Other parts of the Declaration are hortatory in tone, reminiscent of Eric Havelock's analysis of the *Iliad*.[48] Instead of providing for three separate branches of government, the Declaration admonishes: "That the legislative, executive, and supreme judicial powers of government, *ought* to be forever separate and distinct from each other."[49] Instead of stating that laws could be suspended only by the representatives, the Declaration entreats: "That all powers of suspending laws, or the execution of laws, by any authority, without consent of the Representatives of the people, is injurious to their rights, and *ought* not to be exercised."[50] Throughout the Declaration exhortations (using "ought"), not prohibitions, are paired with explanations—all to reinforce and remind an audience accustomed to hearing rather than reading. It served, to adapt Eric Havelock's language, "to memorialise and preserve the social apparatus, the governing mechanism, and the education for leadership and social management."[51]

The body of the constitution itself was largely copied from the constitutions of other states.[52] That fact alone reflects the encroachment of writing into the domain of the oral through one of the important characteristics of a written culture—the ability to transfer information accurately over large distances. At the same time, however, because the structure of the new government was little more than a continuation of that under the Crown, the document merely repeated the established constitutional rules. In one group of sections, however, the constitution does reflect its oral origins—when it lists, in seemingly unnecessary detail, those who are ineligible to hold public office.[53] Gordon Wood accurately captured the effect such a list has on those accustomed to written culture when he wrote that the drafters had "painstakingly enumerated" those who were ineligible.[54] Then, near the end of the document, the oral character re-emerges in the statement that the Declaration of Rights is part of the constitution and "ought never to be violated on any pretence whatsoever."[55]

## II

North Carolina's legislature selected five delegates to the Convention,[56] but only after "some maneuvering and jugling [sic]."[57] The original choices were Governor Richard Caswell, William R. Davie, Willie Jones, Alexander Martin, and Richard Dobbs Spaight. Whatever else may have been involved in the process of selection, the five well reflected the diverse interests in the state. Caswell, Jones, and Martin were likely to oppose any stronger national government. Davie and Spaight favored increasing the powers of the national government. That composition changed when Caswell and Jones declined to serve. Under authority given him by the legislature, the governor then chose two strong nationalists, William Blount and Hugh Williamson, in their place.[58] Although the delegates had been prominent in the public life of North Carolina for some time, their participation in the debates in Philadelphia was anything but stellar.

Blount[59] and Martin[60] seem hardly to have been there at all. At the time of his selection, Blount was one of the state's delegates to the Confederation Congress. On account of illness, he did not arrive in Philadelphia until June 19, taking his seat the next day.[61] He left for New York to attend Congress soon thereafter[62] and missed the entire month of July before returning to Philadelphia for the last month of the Convention.[63] Blount is mentioned only twice in Madison's notes, once when he took his seat and once when he emphasized that his signing meant no more than that the document was the unanimous act of the states at the Convention.[64]

As early as mid-July, Blount had written to Governor Caswell that he was "not in sentiment with [his] Colleagues" because he thought that "we shall ultimately and not many Years first be separated and distinct Governments perfectly independent of each other."[65] Nevertheless, Blount later predicted that the states would ratify the constitution.[66]

Martin had no similar public explanation for his lack of participation, though it is possible that his silence resulted from opposition to the document.[67] He was at the Convention from its formal opening on May 25 through late August.[68] Nevertheless, he garnered only four references, once for attending and the rest for seconding minor motions made by other delegates.[69] Williamson suggested that Martin's lack of participation was the result of his having "so exhausted his fund [while Governor of the state], that time must be required to enable him again to exert his abilities to the advantage of the nation."[70]

Davie[71] and Spaight[72] occasionally entered into debate, but only with brief comments. Davie was at the Convention from its opening through mid-August when he returned to North Carolina to attend a sitting of the superior court.[73] After his return to North Carolina, Davie wrote to Governor Caswell that he "felt [him]self fully at liberty to return" since the "general principles were already fixed . . . [and] especially as No. Carolina was so fully and respectably represented."[74] While at the Convention he served on the Committee of Eleven, or the first Grand Committee, appointed early in July to attempt to resolve the impasse over representation in the two houses of Congress.[75] Davie was one of the strongest supporters of the Constitution in the state convention.[76]

Spaight attended the Convention throughout the summer and signed the draft constitution. He served on no committees. Spaight later served as a delegate to the ratification convention, where he supported the Constitution with modest effort.

Williamson alone was a frequent participant in the debates. Blount described Williamson as the head of the delegation.[77] William Pierce likewise gave Williamson the highest praise of any of the North Carolina delegates: "Mr Williamson is a Gentleman of education and talents. He enters freely into public debate from his close attention to most subjects, but he is no Orator. There is a great degree of good humor and pleasantry in his character; and in his manners there is a strong trait of the Gentleman."[78] In addition to his regular participation in the debates, Williamson served on five committees, the subjects of which were: (1) representation in the House of Representatives; (2) the militia and the assumption of state debts; (3) the interrelated question of navigation acts, imposts, and slavery; (4) navigation acts, a second time; and (5) remaining matters.[79] Williamson signed the document without reservations.[80] He then returned to the Confederation Congress from which he served as an apologist for North Carolina and a defender of the Constitution.[81]

The absence of significant division among the delegates themselves makes it impossible to discern individual preferences.[82] Rarely did they present comprehensive views about the shape of any new national government, possibly because other delegates from the South (Virginia and South Carolina in particular) readily did so.[83] The generally lackluster caliber of what comments they did make affords little insight into the concerns of North Carolina. Furthermore, to the extent that the delegates generally supported the Constitution, they failed to represent the strong opposition among the people of North Carolina, as would be dramatically confirmed during the ratification debates.[84] In the absence of significant participation in the debates, the North Carolinians seemed content to play one of two roles: editorial proofreaders for the Convention or chauvinistic spokesmen for North Carolina. The most that can be said in their favor is that their participation affords a realistic picture of the complexity of the debate.

A more favorable version of the delegates' performance appears in a letter written by the three delegates who remained at the Convention at the end (Blount, Spaight, and Williamson). Doubtless they recognized the letter, which accompanied the proposed Constitution,[85] as the first salvo in the battle over both ratification

and their own performance.[86] The letter, insofar as it anticipates
the most important concerns in the state, shows the state to be
decidedly oriented toward itself. Regional concerns were only
secondary. The delegates began with assurances "that no exertions
have been wanting on our part to guard and promote the particular
interest of North Carolina."[87] Chief among those "particular"
interests was insuring that the specie-poor state not be excessively
burdened by taxation.[88] Their more general goal was to protect an
amorphous "southern" interest. The delegates linked those two
goals when they explained: "We had many things to hope from a
National Government and the chief thing we had to fear from such
a Government was the Risque of unequal or heavy Taxation, but we
hope you will believe as we do that the Southern States in general
and North Carolina in particular are well secured on that head by
the proposed system."[89] Textual restrictions on the power to tax
protected North Carolina while the requirement of a regular
census would prevent the southern states from being over-
whelmed in the House of Representatives,[90] as would the requirement of a two-thirds vote of Senators to ratify treaties.[91]

Mixing the particular interests with the regional, they further
explained that the requirement that direct taxes could be apportioned only according to population was "greatly in our favour" as
compared with the burden on eastern states.[92] They admitted to
having failed to secure North Carolina its full entitlement of representatives in the first House. But, they explained, they had re-
frained from insisting upon a larger number lest it bring with it an
increased tax burden. Almost in passing, they mentioned that
adding three-fifths of the number of slaves to the state's population
would give the state decided advantages over what it had in the
Confederation Congress and that there was better security for
return of fugitive slaves than under confederation.[93]

When the delegates turned to explain what had been the concessions, they tactfully wrote not in terms of particular losses to
North Carolina but of concessions by the southern states in general. The concept of regional identity was inherently worthy of

defense. "While we were taking so much care to guard ourselves against being over reached and to form rules of Taxation that might operate in our favour, it is not to be supposed that our Northern Brethren were Inattentive to their particular Interest."[94] What the northern states got was a navigation act. "[B]ut," Blount, Spaight, and Williamson added, returning to their earlier chauvinism with the most revealing comment in the letter, "we beg leave to observe in the course of this Interchange North Carolina does not appear to us to have given up *anything* for we are doubtless the most independent of the Southern States; we are able to carry our own produce and if the Spirit of Navigation and Ship building is cherished in our State we shall soon be able to carry for our Neighbors."[95]

North Carolina's participation in the Convention, though unimpressive, was not without moments worthy of note. As editors, Spaight and especially Williamson, occasionally showed a keen sense of regard for the success of their venture. For example, at the beginning of the Convention, Spaight offered the very helpful suggestion that no rule should preclude the delegates from reconsidering any vote.[96] On at least three occasions one of the North Carolinians suggested language that later found its way into the Constitution. In mid-summer Williamson offered a thought that eventually allowed the delegates to move away from a stalemate on the question of electing the President. He suggested that each person who voted for President should vote for three people. The process, he suggested, would increase the probability of a vote for a resident of another state.[97] From that suggestion the delegates fashioned the requirement that electors vote for at least one candidate not in their own state.[98]

On September 3, Williamson again helped move the Convention away from a deadlocked position. The issue on this occasion was whether members of Congress should be eligible for other offices. The delegates had struggled unsuccessfully to find language that would bar abuses without unnecessarily limiting the pool of qualified officeholders. Williamson's proposal succeeded in resolving the struggle: no one would be eligible for an office "created or the emoluments whereof shall have been increased" during the term of office.[99] Four days later, Spaight proposed the language that authorizes the President to make recess appointments.[100]

Of considerably more importance were the conciliatory efforts made by North Carolina to keep the Convention together. These efforts echo, but do not directly support, the deductions of scholars including Staughton Lynd and Forrest McDonald who see North Carolina as playing a crucial role in the compromise between northern and southern states over navigation and slavery.[101] It is ironic that North Carolina's lack of development should, on the one hand, dispose it against a strong national government, yet on the other hand, prevent it from having such a strong southern identity that it could not compromise. North Carolina's slow development made its future less certain than states such as South Carolina or Georgia which saw clearly their future as a slave-based, agricultural society. By contrast, and as the delegates had reported to Governor Caswell, North Carolina could see its future as including shipping if conditions warranted.

In the critical period at the end of June and beginning of July, the North Carolina delegates were unusually active participants in urging conciliation. At the end of June the Convention was near a standstill if not dissolution over the structure of the Congress. Davie, who had not spoken before, urged a compromise, observing, "We are partly federal, partly national in our Union, and he did not see why the Gov[ernment] might not in some respects operate on the States, in others on the people."[102] By echoing language used the day before by Oliver Ellsworth of Connecticut, Davie seemed to be signalling that North Carolina (theretofore a member of the large-state bloc) had joined with Connecticut (a member of the small-state bloc) to promote compromise.[103] In spite of Davie's conciliatory language, the North Carolina delegation voted against allowing each state equal representation, in the historic tie vote on July 2.[104] But later the same day Williamson too urged compromise, through the appointment of a committee: "If we do not concede on both sides, our business must soon be at an end."[105] Appropriately, Davie was elected to serve on the committee.[106]

When debate on the compromise (proportional representation in the House; denying the Senate the power to originate money bills; and equal representation in the Senate) became acrimonious, Williamson joined other delegates in calling for calm consideration of the compromise, in spite of his personal dislike for the proposal.[107] There is no conclusive evidence that North Carolina's words or deeds, on or off the floor of the Convention, had any effect. It is true, though, that four days after voting against equality of representation for Senate, the North Carolina delegation joined the small states in voting to retain part of a compromise that included equal representation in the Senate—the provision allowing only the House to originate money bills.[108] North Carolina also voted with the small states to approve the entire compromise.[109] Thereafter, the North Carolina delegates, led by Williamson, staunchly defended the compromise. Later efforts to dilute the compromise[110] elicited the most vehement comment by Williamson during the entire summer. His support, he said, had been "a matter of conscience."[111]

The perseverance of the North Carolina delegates in support of the compromise was not without exception, they did bristle occasionally, especially when confronted with what they perceived to be significant intrusions on the key interests of their state. Less than two weeks after his mollifying comments, Davie rebuked his fellow delegates who sought to deprive the southern states of representation for slaves. "It was," Davie warned, "high time now to speak out. He saw that it was meant by some gentlemen to deprive the Southern States of any share of Representation for their blacks. He was sure that [North Carolina] would never confederate on any terms that did not rate them at least as 3/5. If the Eastern States meant therefore to exclude them altogether the business was at an end."[112] Williamson also favored the three-fifths ratio, but explained his support in more conciliatory terms. The ratio, he said, was not at either extreme; it lay between equality of blacks to whites and inferiority when apportioning taxes.[113] Williamson later explained that he was personally opposed to slavery but thought it "more in favor of humanity, from a view of all circumstances, to let in S.C. & Georgia on those terms, than to exclude them from the Union."[114] Williamson also warned that the southern states would not join without a clause allowing the importation of slaves.[115]

Williamson's comment illustrates the second, and more amorphous, goal identified in the delegates' letter to Governor Caswell: protecting the regional interests of the South. In his case, though, that interest was related to trade as well as slavery. Though not in such abrupt language, Williamson too had told the delegates of the importance of the states but in terms of the need for compromise. He was, he said, "a friend to such a system as would secure the existence of the State [Governments]. The happiness of the people depended on it."[116] Even his suggestion that voters vote for a presidential candidate from another state was designed to protect the interests of the smaller states.[117] It also seems to have been part of his preference for a three-member executive, with one member to represent each of three districts into which the nation would be divided. "As the Executive is to have a kind of veto on the laws, and there is an essential difference of interests between the N. & S. States, particularly in the carrying trade, the power will be dangerous, if the Executive is to be taken from part of the Union, to the part from which he is not taken. The case is different here from what it is in England; where there is a sameness of interests throughout the Kingdom."[118]

The North Carolina delegation, or at least Williamson and Davie, therefore recognized the existence of sectional differences. But in their voting they demonstrated a flexibility which belies a firmly developed *southern* identity. When the scene shifted from Philadelphia to Hillsborough, North Carolina, issues of "southernness" disappeared almost entirely. The delegates to the state constitutional convention concentrated upon the extent to which North Carolina's interests would be compromised by the new government. Freed of the need to protect a regional interest, the delegates exhibited differences which had to that point been unstated, possibly because not represented.

The primary fear of the Antifederalists was that the new national government threatened the autonomy of their local, oral-based communities. They saw delegates from other states not so much as "northern," but as "different." They appreciated, and valued, the flexibility inherent in face-to-face meetings; and they viewed with apprehension the results of such a meeting carried on at a distance from their local, homogeneous audiences.

### III

The mosaic of North Carolina's divisions becomes fully evident, then, only in the debate after the Philadelphia Convention. The basic character of that debate is well known from discussions elsewhere.[119] There is, nonetheless, more to be learned from studying the debates with an emphasis on how they reflect the process of a written culture replacing an oral one. The most pervasive illustration of that process comes from the contrasting ways of dealing with text. There are also revealing disagreements over specific issues, in particular, trial by jury and a meeting place for the new Congress.

Throughout the debate the Federalists exhibited a ready fluency with meaning and interpretation of text. For them one need only look at a dictionary or apply "ordinary" rules of construction to discern the meaning of the Constitution, or any other text. By contrast, the primarily oral Antifederalists had no such understanding.[120] The conservative nature of their oral society found itself opposed to the abstraction that would be the *written* constitution. No longer would human experience constitute the government. Instead, the text would provide the basis for governmental structure, thus separating human experience from government

and introducing the need for rules of construction and interpretation.[121] Furthermore, surrendering the government to a written
text meant surrendering it to "wise" men who understood the rules
for use of the new tool.[122] That for much of backcountry North
Carolina was anathema.

In the months before the North Carolina convention met, this
difference reflected itself in the type of campaign waged by each
side. The well-organized Federalists relied more upon printed
media—pamphlets and the state's few newspapers.[123] The Antifederalists' "campaign was based less on formal organization and
publicity and more on informal intercourse and appeals to the fears
and prejudices as well as to the sober judgment of the people."[124]

In the convention itself, the mnemonic component of the Antifederalists' culture was evident immediately after the delegates
agreed upon rules. Two of the Antifederalists moved the *reading* of
the following: North Carolina's Declaration of Rights and Constitution, the Articles of Confederation, the act authorizing delegates to
Philadelphia, and the resolution from Congress accompanying the
Constitution.[125] Likewise, a day later David Caldwell, a Pres-
byterian minister and Antifederalist delegate, argued that it was
"necessary to lay down such rules or maxims as ought to be the
fundamental principles of every free government; and after laying
down such rules, to compare the Constitution with them, and see
whether it has attended to them; for if it be not founded on such
principles, it cannot be proper for our adoption."[126] Caldwell's
principles[127] epitomized the nature of law in an oral culture:
"[law is] enshrined in formulaic sayings, proverbs, which are not
mere jurisprudential decorations, but themselves constitute the
law."[128] For Caldwell and his Antifederalist colleagues, these
proverbs became the mnemonic by which they judged the law.

The Federalists at the convention saw the maxims as a text to be
analyzed, not as an aid to memory. Since the maxims were not the
text the convention had assembled to consider, the Federalists
opposed Caldwell's proposal. Two of the most powerful Federalists, William R. Davie and James Iredell, urged the convention

not to allow discussion that would only delay their proceedings. Davie, who had been a delegate to the Philadelphia Convention, predicted that "it was highly improbable that they should agree on" the maxims. The disagreement, he explained enigmatically, "arose from the nature of things."[129] Iredell, who would become a member of the first Supreme Court of the United States, urged the rejection of one of Caldwell's maxims based on an analysis of the language itself.[130] In response, an Antifederalist delegate suggested that Iredell was merely "quibbl[ing] upon words."[131] To which Iredell replied in language which epitomized a written culture: "If my premises are wrong, let them be attacked. If my conclusions be wrong, let me be put right. I am sorry that, in debating so important a subject, it could be thought that we were disputing about words."[132]

Antifederalist delegates urged that the Constitution be understood by everyone—their face-to-face society required that speaker and audience alike understand the discourse through participating in the same context. Their urgings drew on a familiar theme, one that had been used in the contest against the Crown a decade earlier. Then too the North Carolinians distinguished between the artificial logic of judicial procedure and the knowledge that could be derived from ordinary experience. "Of the Modes of carrying on the weighty Affairs of State; of the Artifice, Cunning, Address, and Subtility of Courts, it is the general Lot to be ignorant; but of the great Principles of Government, especially of this free State, of those Laws and Proceedings, that are . . . corroborative of the System, many are as liable to judge as any Minister employed in his Majesty's Service."[133] In the convention, William Lenoir asserted that the "most humble and trifling characters in the country have a right to know what foundation they stand upon."[134] Likewise, Joseph McDowall explained that he would "be extremely sorry to live under a government which the people could not understand, and which it would require the greatest abilities to understand. It ought to be plain and easy to the meanest capacity."[135] To the Federalists' rejoinder that the text could be readily construed, the Antifederalists responded by rejecting all dependence upon wise men for learning meaning. Particular doctrines, they argued, "should be expressly declared in the Constitution, and not left to mere construction and opinion."[136]

For the Federalists, who were more comfortable with written texts, there was nothing to fear from construction. They freely referred to the "usual meaning of language,"[137] and "universal principles of jurisprudence."[138] When pressed on the meaning of a provision, they responded as did Davie, with surprise that there could be any doubt about the meaning: "Is this not the plain, literal, and grammatical construction of the clause? Is it possible to put any other construction on it, without departing from the natural order, and without deviating from the general meaning of the words, and every rule of grammatical construction?"[139]

The Antifederalists were unmoved by arguments requiring definitions or grammatical rules; their oral society had need of neither since meaning was evident from the shared context in which both speaker and listener participated.[140] Instead, they preferred the security provided by human experience. William Goudy made the point nicely when he explained that he was "not able to follow these learned gentlemen through all the labyrinths of their oratory. . . . But," he continued, "I have a judgment of my own; and, though not so well informed always as others, yet I will exert it when manifest danger presents itself. . . . Gentlemen, by their learned arguments, endeavor to conceal the danger from us. I have no notion of this method of evading arguments, and of clouding them over with rhetoric, and, I must say, sophistry too."[141] Goudy's response is symptomatic of the disruption that can be caused by the introduction of a written text. In the words of Brian Stock, the new text, "transforms man's conception of himself in society. . . . One no longer responds through inherited principles handed down by word of mouth. The model is now exteriorized. Individual experience still counts, but its role is delimited; instead, loyalty and obedience are given to a more or less standardized set of rules which lie outside the sphere of influence of the person, the family, or the community."[142]

The Antifederalists revealed their discomfort in dealing with a written document in yet another way. Because they saw the document in an aggregative way, as a list of discrete items preserved for the sake of memory, they tended to object to single provisions, taken in isolation from the rest of the document. For example, they objected to the provision that the "Senate shall have the sole Power to try all Impeachments."[143] To them "sole" meant that no state legislature or any agency of a state could try an impeachment.[144]

Each of the specific objections was palpably wrong in the opinion of the Federalists. To them it was plain that when "several clauses relate to the same subject [they] ought to be considered together."[145] They would also appeal to "a maxim of universal jurisprudence, or reason and common sense" to show that "an instrument or deed *of writing* shall be so construed as to give validity to all parts of it, if it can be done without involving any absurdity."[146]

The debate on Caldwell's maxims was but a preview of the key substantive debate of the convention, that about a bill of rights. The Antifederalists repeatedly insisted upon the need for a bill of rights, a mnemonic, to enable the people to know when their rights were violated. The Federalists responded with exegesis of the text to show that a bill of rights was unnecessary. To the Antifederalists, a bill of rights offered a way of controlling the text of the Constitution. A bill of rights, in the words of McDowell, provided the opportunity "to see every thing fixed."[147] The value in such a statement was like the value in periodically walking the limits of a field. Written records might be lost or even forged, but the process of walking the boundaries called upon the collective community memory and experience to validate the claim.[148] Based on their actual experience, the Antifederalists knew that what was true for a field was equally true for a constitution: "if a boundary were set up, when the boundary is passed, the people would take notice of it immediately."[149] For the Antifederalists, the mnemonic bill of rights contained words with only the latest, definite meaning. Earlier meanings would have been discarded from the usage of their oral culture. Thus words were as definite as the posts and beams in a boundary fence, apparent to even the "most humble and trifling characters."[150]

But to the Federalists, words were abstract concepts subject to analysis and rules of construction. The Federalists, too, could draw upon experiences. But these experiences were the rules that evolved from abstracting written texts. The text itself was, to use one of their metaphors, like a "power of attorney" under which only those powers granted could be exercised. To create a bill of rights would activate another principle of construction that would lead to the implication that those rights not listed were not preserved.[151] The *written* Constitution itself, with its rules for construction, would be sufficient safeguard for the rights of the people.[152]

The most important of the components of a bill of rights was the guarantee of a trial by jury. As "An Independent Citizen" wrote in a broadside addressed to Davie, nothing could "save him from destruction" but "an impartial trial by a *jury of his neighbours* well acquainted with him and his cause, and the malignity of his accusers."[153] Two of the characterizations in that phrase suggest the oral culture in which the author lived. The jurors were, first, "neighbors," and, second, already "well acquainted" with the writer and his accuser. These jurors were, therefore, essential precisely because they were fully aware of the context in which events had occurred. Their participation in the oral, face-to-face culture made them uniquely capable of resolving disputes.

The Federalists' response revealed both their internalization of a written culture and the threat which that culture posed to the localistic communities of the Antifederalists. According to the Federalists, there could be no provision for trial by jury because of the great differences among the states.[154] Those differences made it impossible for a single phrase, "trial by jury," to have the same meaning regardless of context. Thus the phrase could not be included in a written constitution.

The Federalists' argument triggered a two-fold response. One was to observe that if the states had such different concepts of the jury then "the genius of the people of the United States is so dissimilar that our liberties cannot be secured, we can never hang long together. Interest is the band of social union; and when this is taken away, the Union itself must dissolve."[155] The other response was to note that the insistence upon a common meaning confirmed that the Federalists sought a consolidated government which would destroy the states by insisting upon uniformity throughout the nation.[156]

In addition to the absence of a bill of rights, the other of the Antifederalists' great fears was for the consequences of a Congress meeting at a distance from North Carolina. The different context would provide no stability for meaning, no assurance that the local interests of North Carolina would be protected. As McDowall warned: "At such a distance from their homes, and for so long a time, they will have no feeling for, nor any knowledge of, the situation of the people."[157] Another Antifederalist, Joseph Taylor, drew on tangible experience to make a similar point: "The man who has a large estate cannot manage it with convenience. I conceive that, in the present case, a consolidated government can by no means suit the genius of the people."[158] As a final example, Judge Spencer, used the specific example of taxation to make the same point. The "most certain criterion of happiness that any people can have," he said, "is to be taxed by their own immediate representatives,—by those representatives who intermix with them, and know their circumstances,—not by those who cannot know their situation. Our federal representatives cannot sufficiently know our situation and circumstances."[159] Their immediate experience caused them to recall what happened when delegates from each state had assembled in the new context (convention) in Philadelphia. The Antifederalists' pointed rhetorical question was "If the best characters departed so far from their authority, what may not be apprehended from others, who may be agents in the new government?"[160]

The Federalists had no effective response to that complaint.

Davie's description of the "people of the United States [as having] one common interest [and being] all members of the same community,"[161] was simply contrary to the experiences of the Antifederalists. Whitmill Hill urged that the representatives be trusted because they "go from us—are situated like ourselves."[162] Johnston likewise pled for trust: "The men of whom Congress will consist are to be chosen from among ourselves. They will be in the same situation with us. They are to be bone of our bone and flesh of our flesh. They cannot injure us without injuring themselves."[163] Hill and Johnston, like most of the other Federalists, failed to appreciate the nature of the Antifederalists' fear of representatives meeting at a distance from their original, shared locale.

## IV

When the North Carolina antifederalists insisted on a bill of rights they responded to a written document in the only way they knew—they tried to make it record the oral tradition. The Antifederalists agreed not so much on the content of the list of rights as on the need to have it as a constant reminder, a mnemonic, for their aural citizens. North Carolina, therefore, well illustrates the transitional nature of American society in the late eighteenth century: poised between an agricultural past and an industrial future; and poised between a fading oral culture and an emerging written one.

# "The Good Old Cause": The Ratification of the Constitution and Bill of Rights in South Carolina

JAMES W. ELY, JR.

The history of South Carolina during the 1780s is primarily a story of recovery from the Revolutionary War. The Revolutionary struggle in the Palmetto State was particularly savage and destructive, leaving "the state impoverished with its treasury empty, its commerce nearly destroyed, and many of its citizens heavily in debt."[1] When the British left Charleston late in 1782, Carolinians faced a bleak scene of ruined plantations and a disorganized slave labor force. The departing British stole some 25,000 slaves, about one fourth of the state's work force.[2] Agriculture was crippled by this loss of labor. The closing of trade with the British West Indies contributed to the decline of the port of Charleston. The currency was debased, credit virtually extinct, and manufactured products scarce. Crop failures in 1784 and 1785 aggravated the depressed economic picture. The export of rice, the state's principal staple crop, fell off dramatically.[3] South Carolina thus began its independence with many members of the dominant planter class under a tremendous burden of debt.

The principal political controversies in the state during these years resulted from the war and the depressed economic conditions. Because planters and legislators were prominent among the debtor class, they did not hesitate to seek government protection. Throughout the 1780s the assembly repeatedly intervened in creditor-debtor relations with a host of stay laws, installment payment acts, and measures regulating attachments and sheriffs' sales.[4] In 1785, when the hard times were most acute, the legislature responded with the famous property tender law—termed the Pine Barren Act by critics—which was designed to frustrate the collection of debts.[5]

Under the pressure of economic distress, politically influential groups in the state legislature invariably acted with favor upon congressional requests for increased powers. It approved the imposts of 1781 and 1783, for example, as well as the requests by Congress for authority to regulate foreign trade. Agents of the Congress were granted authority to sue in the state courts for the recovery of debts owed the United States.[6] The statutes of the decade ring with such phrases as "the safety, honour and interest of the United States of America, require . . ." and "as shall appear most for the general interest and welfare of the said States."[7]

Consequently, when Congress in 1786 called for a convention to revise the Articles of Confederation the Palmetto State was quick to respond. South Carolina's position favoring union was clearly expressed in the act appointing delegates to the Philadelphia convention in 1787. After asserting that the powers of Congress were "greatly inadequate" and that the Articles of Confederation needed revision, the statute noted:

> [T]his state is, and ever hath been, ready and willing to co-operate with the other States in union, in devising and adopting such measures as will most effectively insure the peace and general welfare of the confederacy.[8]

These measures foreshadowed the strongly Federalist position of the state's political leadership in the battle over the ratification of the federal constitution.[9]

I

In March of 1787 the South Carolina legislature elected John Rutledge, Charles Coatesworth Pinckney, Charles Pinckney, and Pierce Butler to represent the state at the Philadelphia convention "for the purpose of revising the Federal Constitution."[10] By any standard this was an able delegation.[11] All were experienced political figures who had served in the state legislature. Rutledge had been governor of the Palmetto State during the Revolutionary War, and C.C. Pinckney was a Brigadier General. Further, Charles Pinckney, Rutledge, and Butler had represented South Carolina in Congress under the Articles of Confederation.[12] All were lawyers except Butler. Born a member of the Anglo-Irish aristocracy, Butler had moved to Charleston before the Revolution and married into a prominent South Carolina family. He was a planter who owned several large plantations.[13]

At the same time, the selection of the delegates underscored economic and geographic divisions within the Palmetto State. All members of the delegation were residents of Charleston and vicinity.[14] Moreover, all were wealthy slave owners. In short, the low country elite completely dominated the Carolina delegation, to exclusion of any voice on behalf of the more numerous small farmers of the back country.[15]

As this common background suggests, there was a high degree of unanimity among the delegates. The vain and ambitious Charles Pinckney, at 29 one of the youngest member of the Philadelphia convention, emerged as the informal leader of the South Carolinians. Indeed, following presentation of the famous Virginia Plan by Edmund Randolph, Charles Pinckney offered his own plan for a federal government. The Pinckney proposal was similar to the Virginia Plan, and was never formally considered by the convention.[16] Despite this disappointment, Charles Pinckney participated heavily in debate and many of his recommendations were adopted as part of the Constitution.[17] Both Rutledge and Butler also spoke often, and Rutledge was a member of the important Committee of Detail, the body which prepared a working draft of the Constitution. Professor Lander has aptly concluded: "With the exception of the Virginia and Pennsylvania delegations, the South Carolina delegation was second to none in importance at Philadelphia."[18]

The South Carolinians worked to achieve a strong central government which would be under the control of a propertied elite. Like most delegates, they wanted a new government capable of paying public debts, establishing a sound commercial policy, and protecting property interests. Specifically, they favored a single term of office for the President, a House of Representatives elected by the state legislatures, and a Congress in which both houses were apportioned according to total population, slave as well as free. Rutledge successfully proposed adoption of the supremacy clause whereby the Constitution, federal statutes, and treaties were declared to be the supreme law in the states.[19] South Carolina's delegates also voted to strengthen the powers of Congress. Indeed, Charles Pinckney, the most nationalistic member of the delegation, moved that "the National Legislature should have authority to negative all Laws which they should judge to be improper."[20] Despite a second by James Madison, this broad power was too much for most delegates. It was defeated by a wide margin.

Notwithstanding their support for a strengthened national government, the South Carolinians wanted to maintain a balance between state and federal power, and wished to safeguard the basic rights of the people. Their attitude was best expressed by C.C. Pinckney, who declared his preference "to have a good national Govt. & at the same time to leave a considerable share of power in the States."[21] Concerned to protect civil liberties, Charles Pinckney offered a series of resolutions which constituted an incipient bill of rights. He sought to protect freedom of the press, to prohibit religious tests as a condition of holding office, to curtail peacetime quartering of troops, and to guarantee the writ of habeas corpus.[22] Pinckney's proposals were referred to the Committee of Detail, and were never considered by the convention. Not easily discouraged, Pinckney pursued his efforts to protect civil liberties. The convention eventually adopted Pinckney's motions on the suspension of habeas corpus and the prohibition of religious tests.[23] His resolution "that the liberty of the Press shall be inviolably observed" was rejected, however, with opponents reasoning that Congress had no power over the press and hence this protection was unnecessary.[24]

On several important issues the South Carolina delegates were at odds with the majority at the convention. For instance, the South Carolinians joined three other states in opposing equal representation in the Senate, a matter that was at the heart of the constitutional compromise on representation.[25] Furthermore, the Carolina delegation unsuccessfully attempted to prevent the establishment of lower federal courts, arguing that state courts should exercise original jurisdiction in most cases.[26] Anxious to protect southern economic interests from domination by New England shipping, Charles Pinckney moved that a two-thirds vote of each house of Congress be necessary to regulate commerce. Deserted even by his colleagues, Pinckney saw his proposal defeated.[27]

The South Carolinians had their greatest impact on the formation of the Constitution in the area of slavery. They worked steadily to secure the rights of masters to recapture fugitive slaves, to allow continuation of the slave trade, and to count slaves as a basis of Congressional representation. The numerous provisions of the Constitution that sustain slavery attest to the determination of the South Carolina delegates. As William M. Wiecek has observed, "slavery was more clearly and explicitly established under the Constitution than it had been under the Articles."[28]

South Carolina's delegates achieved substantial concessions in face of a tepid anti-slavery sentiment shared by most members of the convention. They made no attempt to defend slavery on moral grounds, but cited historical, political, and economic reasons for its existence. "If slavery be wrong," Charles Pinckney declared, "it is justified by the example of all the world." Noting the examples of ancient Greece and Rome, Pinckney boldly concluded: "In all ages one half of mankind have been slaves."[29] Likewise, John Rutledge stated: "Religion & humanity had nothing to do with this question—Interest alone is the governing principle with Nations."[30]

Slavery became intertwined with the vexing issue of representation in the new Congress. Reflecting the ambiguous legal position of slaves as both persons and property, the three-fifths compromise was not entirely illogical. Although less than the South Carolinians desired, the three-fifths clause was a significant boost for the slave states. Not only did the provision represent an acknowledgement of slavery, but it guaranteed additional political clout for slave states in the House of Representatives.[31]

Regulation of the international slave trade prompted an occasionally bitter debate. Virginians joined New Englanders in demanding an end to or a duty upon imported slaves. To forestall these proposals, the South Carolinians threatened disunion should the convention adopt restrictions on the slave trade. Hence, Rutledge stressed the underlying political issue: "The true question at present is whether the Southn. States shall or shall not be parties to the Union."[32] C.C. Pinckney echoed this view, warning that if he and "all his colleagues were to sign the Constitution & use their personal influence, it would be of no avail towards obtaining the assent of their Constituents. S. Carola. & Georgia cannot do without slaves." He added that suggested restrictions on the slave trade would constitute "an exclusion of S. Carola from the Union."[33] These tactics proved effective. Anxious above all to obtain national union, the delegates accepted a compromise which prevented Congress from prohibiting the slave trade until 1808. In turn, the lower South agreed that a simple majority of Congress could control commerce and navigation.[34]

The rendition of fugitive slaves was also a concern of the South Carolina delegation. Pierce Butler was instrumental in securing adoption of a fugitive slave provision. There was surprisingly little discussion of this measure, and the motion passed unanimously.[35] Historians have explained this action by the convention as a further concession to the South in exchange for allowing a simple majority of Congress to regulate commerce.[36]

The South Carolina delegation was therefore primarily responsible for placing guarantees of slavery into the Constitution. These provisions, which posed some problems of interpretation, set the stage for acrimonious sectional conflict in future years. Moreover, the convention debates illustrated certain attitudes which came to characterize southern constitutional thought before the Civil War. First, southerners increasingly demanded federal support for the institution of slavery. Second, southerners were prepared to employ talk of disunion as a means to force compromise settlements. Eventually, of course, these threatening tactics lost their efficacy, but such developments are beyond the scope of this paper.

As the Philadelphia convention drew to a close, several delegates from other states refused to sign the proposed Constitution. This prompted both Pinckneys to make strong statements of support.[37] Opposing a suggested second convention, Charles Pinckney dramatically posed "the danger of a general confusion, and an ultimate decision by the Sword" if the Constitution should fail.[38] Despite misgivings on some points, the entire South Carolina delegation favored the adoption of the Constitution.

When the convention adjourned in September of 1787 Charles Pinckney returned to New York and resumed his seat in the Congress of the Confederation.[39] There he joined with convention delegates from other states to persuade Congress to recommend that the proposed Constitution be submitted to a convention in each state for ratification or rejection.[40] In addition, Pinckney published a pamphlet in which he discussed the defects of the Articles of Confederation and set forth his views concerning the formation of a new government.[41] C.C. Pinckney was optimistic about the Constitution, and predicted: "I make no doubt that it will be soon adopted by a large Majority of the states."[42]

Proponents of the new Constitution in South Carolina lost no time in marshalling expressions of popular support. In November a meeting of Chowan County, North Carolina, residents adopted a resolution providing:

> That in the opinion of this meeting, this state can have no prospect either of security or honor, but by a firm and indissoluble union with the other states in the Confederation.[43]

Likewise, the Charleston papers also reported that the Grand Jury for Edenton District, North Carolina expressed its support for the Constitution. Decrying "the disordered and distracted state in which the affairs of the union have been for a long time past," the grand jurors declared: "We admire in the new constitution a proper jealousy of liberty mixed with a due regard to the necessity of a strong authoritative government." They called for the legislature to schedule a convention "on as early a day as possible."[44]

## II

The proposed federal Constitution was the most pressing order of business when the South Carolina legislature met in January of 1788. Governor Thomas Pinckney, who considered the "Federal Union as an object of first magnitude," formally presented the Constitution and the Congressional resolution to the legislators.[45] The Governor's message was referred to a House committee, which unanimously recommended the election of delegates to a state convention to approve or reject the Constitution. The committee's report prompted three days of debate between proponents and critics of the new governmental scheme. Charles Pinckney led the speakers in favor of adoption, while Rawlins Lowndes, a wealthy but maverick Charlestonian, was the principal opposition spokesman.[46] This was the first of what was, in effect, two debates over the ratification of the Constitution in South Carolina. Since the arguments advanced by the contending parties were similar in both debates, it is most convenient to treat them together for the purpose of analyzing the intellectual aspects of the ratification struggle.

After discussing the Constitution in detail the House of Representatives voted unanimously to convene a state ratifying convention.[47] However, a subsequent motion to hold the convention in Charleston on May 12 exposed the sharp divisions within the Palmetto State. Federalists were anxious to gain the tactical advantages of time and place. A quick election would hamper the ability of Antifederalists to organize an effective opposition. Moreover, sentiment in Charleston strongly favored ratification of the Constitution, and the Federalists could use such overwhelming public opinion to influence wavering delegates. Viewed in a broad context, the question of where to hold the convention was part of a struggle between planters and merchants from the low country farmers over control of state government. Although Charleston was still the seat of government in 1788, the back country forces had succeeded in passing an act to build a new capitol at Columbia.[48] Construction of the new capitol was in progress, however, and Charleston remained the most logical site for the convention. Even so, the back country legislators, perhaps sensing the political dangers of selecting Charleston, voted solidly against the motion to convene there. The Federalists must have been relieved when the House, by a 76–75 margin, adopted the motion.[49]

Those favoring ratification enjoyed other political advantages as well. The legislature directed that "such of the Inhabitants of this State as are [entitled] to Vote for Representatives to the General Assembly" should select convention delegates in an April election.[50] Under the South Carolina Constitution of 1778 suffrage was limited to males who owned a freehold of 50 acres or a town lot, or who paid taxes.[51] It has been estimated that more than half of South Carolina males could meet these property qualification,[52] but obviously the less affluent residents would have no direct voice in the ratification process.

Furthermore, representation in the convention, based upon apportionment in the legislature, was heavily weighted in favor of the low country districts. The population of the back country grew steadily after the Revolution, producing a great disparity between population and representation. By the time of the convention a majority of whites lived in the back country. Yet under the apportionment formula as little as 20 percent of the white population could elect a majority of the lawmakers.[53] Consequently, the South Carolina ratifying convention was among the most unequally apportioned, and the costal regions held a disproportionate amount of influence.[54] Since, as we shall see, opposition to the Constitution centered in the back country, the representation provisions significantly skewed the ratification process. In the face of political domination by the low country elite Antifederalist efforts to defeat the Constitution were probably doomed from the outset.

Moreover, the Federalists continued their campaign to influence popular opinion. The Beaufort District Grand Jury urged adoption of the Constitution, declaring that the Constitution was "dictated by the same spirit of liberty which brought about the revolution" and "has every safeguard which human foresight can suggest for perpetuating the blessings of freedom, tranquility, union, and the prosperity of the whole."[55] Dr. David Ramsay, the early historian of the Palmetto State, wrote *An Address to the Freemen of South Carolina on the Federal Constitution* in which he stressed the need for greater unity among the states.[56]

Statements in support of the Constitution, published under pseudonyms, were regularly carried in the Charleston press. For instance, "A Back Wood's Man" attacked "the empty harangues of self important demagogues" who opposed the Constitution and predicted prosperity under the new government.[57] Only rarely did Antifederalist sentiment appear in print.[58] This may reflect the strongly pro-ratification views of Charleston residents and newspapers, but it also indicates that the Antifederalists made little attempt to shape public attitudes. The course of the ratification debates in other states was fully covered in the Charleston newspapers. Indeed, the news that Maryland had become the seventh state to ratify was received while the South Carolina convention was in session, greatly discouraging the Antifederalists.

The convention assembled, as scheduled, in Charleston on May 12, 1788. All of the Philadelphia delegates were elected to the ratifying convention, except for Pierce Butler, who declined to serve.[59] Governor Thomas Pinckney was elected President, and presided over the sessions. The first order of business was to adopt rules to govern the proceedings and to resolve some unsettled delegate elections. It was decided to discuss the proposed Constitution paragraph by paragraph, and then vote on the document as a whole. This procedure prevented the Antifederalists from seeking to attach amendments or conditions to particular articles.[60]

Political matters were not the only things on the minds of delegates. Charleston was suffering from an outbreak of smallpox. A delegate from Fairfield County declined to attend the convention "on account of the small pox being in Charleston and he having never had it."[61] At the request of the convention, John F. Grimke, the Intendant of Charleston, issued a proclamation which urged city inhabitants to keep family members afflicted with smallpox out of the streets "for the satisfaction and security of such of the members of the convention as have not hitherto had the said disorder."[62]

As in the earlier legislative session, Charles Pinckney opened the debate with a speech urging ratification. Rather than examine the course of the legislative and convention debates, this paper will focus on the principal contentions advanced by supporters and critics of the Constitution. Many of these arguments were similar to those set forth elsewhere during the national ratification battle, and thus do not warrant extensive comment here.

Federalists repeatedly ridiculed the inefficiency of Congress under the Articles of Confederation, and blamed inadequate government for loss of credit and decay of commerce. The Confederation, Ramsay maintained, "can neither protect us at home, not gain us respect abroad; it cannot secure the payment of our debts, nor command the resources of our country, in case of danger."[63] Those favoring ratification stressed the following reasons for a strong central government:

1) That it would enable the United States to deal more effectively with foreign governments and to protect American interests overseas.

2) That it would facilitate the restoration of credit and would encourage commerce.

3) That it would offer protection against insurrection and foreign invasion.

The impact of the proposed Constitution upon commerce was discussed at length. Charles Pinckney considered Section 10 of Article I, containing the contracts clause and other constraints upon the states, to be "the soul of the Constitution."

> . . . how much will this section tend to restore your credit with foreigners—to rescue your national character from that contempt which must ever follow the most flagrant violations of public faith and private honesty! No more shall paper money, no more shall tender-laws, drive their commerce from our shores, and darken the American name in every country where it is known. [64]

In a similar vein, C.C. Pinckney defended the prohibition against states issuing paper currency. According to Pinckney, paper money "had corrupted the morals of the people; it had diverted them from the paths of honest industry to the ways of ruinous speculation; it had destroyed both public and private credit. . . ." [65] Ramsay added that the clause prohibiting paper money and the impairment of contract "will doubtless bear hard on debtors who wish to defraud their creditors, but it will be real service to the honest part of the community." [66]

Federalists also emphasized that the Palmetto State was too weak either to remain independent or to join with just the southern states. For instance, C.C. Pinckney argued:

> Without union with the other states, South Carolina must soon fall. Is there any one among us so much a Quixote as to suppose that this state could long maintain her independence if she stood alone, or was only connected with the Southern States? [67]

He stressed that the navy based in New England would protect South Carolina in the event of invasion. Ramsay echoed this theme, contending that "we are inadequate to secure ourselves from more powerful neighbors." [68]

Although they lost no opportunity to extol the virtues of the Constitution, Federalists found it necessary to counter numerous objections raised by adversaries of the proposed new government. Thus, it is particularly instructive to examine the principal criticisms leveled by the Antifederalists.

As in other states, the absence of a Bill of Rights was noted by several speakers. James Lincoln of Ninety-Six District asked: "Why was not this Constitution ushered in with the bill of rights? Are the people to have no rights?"[69] Another delegate declared that the people of Prince Frederick Parish were opposed to the Constitution because "they have omitted to insert a bill of rights therein, ascertaining and fundamentally establishing the unalienable rights of men. . . ."[70] Antifederalists specifically expressed concern about freedom of the press and the right of trial by jury in civil cases.

Opponents also voiced alarm that the interests of South Carolina and the South generally would suffer under the new government. Arguing that the North would politically dominate the union, Antifederalists played upon the fear that the South was a minority section.[71] Rawlins Lowndes dramatically concluded that "when this new Constitution should be adopted, the sun of the Southern States would set, never to rise again."[72] He further observed that no President was "likely ever to be chosen from South Carolina or Georgia."[73] Similarly, Patrick Dollard warned that the Constitution was "big with political mischiefs, and pregnant with a greater variety of impending woes to the good people of the Southern States, especially South Carolina, than all the plagues suppose to issue from the poisonous box of Pandora."[74]

This unhappiness about the place of South Carolina under the Constitution was closely linked to fears that Congress might interfere with slavery. Lowndes attacked the provision which authorized Congress to halt the slave trade in 1808, and observed: "Negroes were our wealth, our only natural resource; yet behold how our kind friends in the north were determined soon to tie up our hands, and drain us of what we had!"[75] The defensive tone adopted by the Federalists in explaining the provisions on slavery suggests that insufficient protection of slave property was a major Antifederalist argument. As Ramsay explained, critics "say that the northern States have no business to interfere with our importation of negroes."[76]

In addition, many opponents of ratification perceived a tendency inherent in the Constitution to foster an aristocracy. James Lincoln alleged that the Constitution would produce "a haughty, imperious aristocracy; and ultimately, a tyrannical monarchy."[77] Another critic charged that the proposed new government "is particularly calculated for the meridian of despotic aristocracy; that it evidently tends to promote the ambitious views of a few able and designing men, and enslave the rest."[78] Fear of elite control of the federal government permeated the Antifederalist viewpoint. This was a sensitive issue because it echoed popular concern that an unrepresentative aristocracy dominated South Carolina's legislature during the 1780s.[79] Much of the Antifederalist alarm focused particularly on the power of the President, and the alleged ease with which the President could assume monarchical authority. The eligibility of the President for re-election was seen as a vehicle for one individual to achieve such undue power.[80]

Furthermore, Lowndes assailed the provision that "all Treaties made . . . under the Authority of the United States, shall be the supreme Law of the Land."[81] He maintained that this measure would not only enhance the power of the President, but that it would effectively repeal South Carolina's installment law for the payment of debts.[82]

Lastly, the Antifederalists claimed that a majority of the people opposed ratification. Alexander Tweed of Prince Frederick Parish, who was persuaded by the debates to support the Constitution, admitted that "the general voice of the people is against it."[83] This caused several critics to assert that the general populace would resist implementation of the new governmental scheme. Lowndes warned against "the adoption of a government which perhaps might require the bayonet to enforce it."[84] Another Antifederalist, describing the attitudes of his constituents, raised a dire threat of forcible hostility:

> They say they will resist against it; that they will not accept of it unless compelled by force of arms, which this new Constitution plainly threatens; and then, they say, your standing army like Turkish janizaries enforcing despotic laws, must ram it down their throats with the points of bayonets. [85]

Proponents of the Constitution endeavored to counter these charges, and two areas deserve particular attention. C.C. Pinckney took the lead in reassuring South Carolinians about the protection of slavery by the Constitution. He pictured the three-fifths clause as a concession by the northern states which recognized slave property for the purpose of determining Congressional representation. [86] Noting that some states favored an immediate cessation of the international slave trade, Pinckney emphasized that "we have secured an unlimited importation of negroes for twenty years." [87] Indeed, Federalists suggested that Congress might not prohibit the slave trade even after 1808. Rejecting any notion that Congress might interfere with domestic slavery, Pinckney explained: "We have a security that the general government can never emancipate them, for no such authority is granted; and it is admitted on all hands, that the general government has no powers but what are expressly granted by the Constitution. . . ." [88] Pinckney also stressed the right to recover fugitive slaves, and concluded: ". . . considering all circumstances, we have made the best terms for the security of this species of property it was in our power to make." [89]

The absence of a bill of rights posed some tactical difficulties for the Federalists. South Carolina's delegates had urged, with only partial success, the formal declaration of certain rights during the Philadelphia convention. Consequently, the arguments of the Antifederalists could not be dismissed out of hand. Charles Pinckney stated that he still thought it would have been desirable to safeguard specifically freedom of the press and the jury trial in civil cases.[90] Nonetheless, he advanced the standard Federalist argument that a bill of rights was unnecessary[91] because the federal government could not deprive the citizens of freedom of the press or interfere with religion.[92]

C.C. Pinckney raised other objections to a bill of rights. Observing that the South Carolina Constitution did not contain such a declaration,[93] he expressed concern that by enumerating certain rights it might be assumed that others were waived.[94] Pinckney then added a most revealing argument:

> Such bills generally begin with declaring that all men are by nature born free. Now, we should make that declaration with a very bad grace, when a large part of our property consists in men who are actually born slaves.[95]

This turned the tables on the Antifederalists, and intimated that a bill of rights might serve to weaken the legal base of slavery.

Following six days of debate, General Thomas Sumter moved to postpone further consideration of the Constitution until mid-October. He was evidently hoping to delay a decision until after the outcome of the Virginia convention, at which the Antifederalists were thought to command a majority. After a spirited debate the motion was defeated by a wide margin, 135 to 89.[96] Realizing the significance of this vote, the spectators in the gallery broke into applause.

Perhaps as a sop to Antifederalist opinion, the convention on the next day appointed a committee to prepare constitutional amendments that should be recommended to Congress. Asserting that "the following amendments would tend to remove the apprehensions of some of the good people of this state, and confirm the blessings intended by the said constitution", the committee recommended approval of four amendments.[97] Most of these amendments reflected the sensitive states rights issue. Thus, one proposal declared that the federal government should not regulate the manner and time of elections except where the states neglected to do so. Another resolution provided that Congress could not levy a direct tax until Congress made a requisition upon the state government and the state refused to pay.[98] The most important proposed amendment broadly stated that, "the states respectively, do retain every power not expressly delegated by this constitution to the general government of the union."[99] This measure would eventually be incorporated into the 10th Amendment to the Constitution. The Antifederalists sought in vain to enlarge the committee report with additional amendments. Judge Aedanus Burke moved to declare that the eligibility of the President for re-election "is dangerous to the Liberties of the people." His proposal was rejected by a tally of 139 to 68.[100] A motion that the militia should not be sent outside of the state without the consent of the consent of the Governor was defeated by voice vote.[101] Once the committee report was adopted as submitted, the opponents of the Constitution made one final effort to modify the document. John Bowman of St. James' Parish, Santee moved that a committee be named to draw up a bill of rights which would be offered as an amendment.[102] The defeat of this resolution set the stage for the decision on ratification.

It can hardly have been a surprise when the convention voted 149 to 73 in favor of ratification.[103] The large Charleston delegation unanimously championed the Constitution, and it enjoyed overwhelming backing from low country members. Ratification received scattered support in the back country, but most delegates from that section were Antifederalists.[104]

News of the convention's action was greeted with great enthusiasm by proponents of the Constitution. In Charleston there was a parade and outdoor dinner to celebrate ratification. The Charleston *City Gazette* reported that "planting and mercantile gentlemen were exceedingly numerous and respectable. . . ."[105] After dining upon a roasted ox the guests enjoyed viewing illuminated ships in the harbor.[106] From across the Palmetto State came similar reports of marches, dinners, patriotic toasts, and symbolic launchings of model federal ships.[107]

Although arguments over the proposed Constitution consumed

several days, the outcome never appeared to be in serious doubt. Three weeks before the convention assembled David Ramsay wrote: "I am pretty confident it will be ratified."[108] Indeed, there was a shadow-boxing quality to the entire convention and the discussions, as reported, seem rather listless. As Edward Rutledge explained to John Jay:

> We had a tedious but trifling opposition to contend with. We had prejudices to contend with and sacrifices to make. Yet they were worth making for the good old cause.[109]

Despite jubilation in Federalist circles, hostility to the convention Judge Burke, a prominent Antifederalist, maintained that "4/5 of the people do, from their souls detest it." He added: "In the interior country, all is disgust, sorrow, and vindictive reproaches against the system. . . ."[110] Historians have likewise concluded that probably a majority of South Carolinians were against ratification.[111] By any standard, then, the Federalists engineered a remarkable achievement by securing adoption of the Constitution in the face of widespread enmity.

A number of factors account for the Federalist success. Inequality of representation at the convention and the proratificaton stance of the press aided that course of ratification. One authority has concluded that the South Carolina delegates favoring the Constitution represented only 39% of the white population.[112] In addition, the Federalists benefited from the superior social and political prestige of their leaders. According to Burke, "[a]ll the rich, leading men, along the seacoast and rice settlements; with few exceptions, lawyers, physicians and divines, the merchants, mechanicks, the populace, and mob of Charleston" favored the Constitution.[113] South Carolina Antifederalists, on the other hand, were largely local figures without substantial influence. Patrick Dollard, for instance, was a tavern keeper.[114]

Another important element was the lack of organization by the Antifederalists. There is no evidence that opponents sought to work in concert or develop strategies, and certainly they could not begin to match the extensive communications network of the Federalists. Moreover, proponents of the Constitution were strengthened by the rapid ratification in other states. This generated a sense of momentum which convinced many that adoption was inevitable, and hence serious opposition futile.

The role of Charleston in the ratification struggle requires special attention. Burke felt that "the principal cause" for the Federalist victory "was holding the Convention in the City, where there are not fifty inhabitants who are not friendly to it."[115] As this suggests, there were no class lines division in Charleston on this issue. Artisans and mechanics generally supported the Constitution in the hope of gaining protection against foreign commerce.[116] Lavish hospitality was extended to convention delegates, providing agreeable opportunities to impress or persuade Antifederalists from rural area. "The merchants and leading men," Burke complained, "kept open houses for the back and low country members during the whole time the Convention sat."[117] Although it is difficult to assess the impact of such informal inducements, there is no doubt that Charleston was at the pinnacle of its importance in South Carolina politics. With only slight exaggeration Professor George Rogers has observed: "Without the city, the state would not have been for ratification."[118]

The division over the Constitution in South Carolina was largely along commercial versus non-commercial lines. The Federalists represented urban centers, the learned professions, mercantile interests, creditors, and planters who were producing crops for export. In contrast, Antifederalists spoke for small farmers, debtors, and back country areas less concerned with business.[119] Ramsay, for instance, identified resistance to the Constitution with debtors. "Some considerable opposition," he noted, "is expected from the favorers of instalment laws valuation laws pine barren laws & legal tender paper laws."[120] Thus, the obvious sectional split in the Palmetto State also reflected socio-economic distinctions. This, however, is not the full story. These class differences were exacerbated by general resentment in the back country against the undue influence of the low country elite over state government. The ratification struggle was also part of a sectional battle for political supremacy, which included the relocation of the capitol and the movement for a state constitutional convention in 1790.[121]

### III

The Palmetto State played only a secondary role in formulating the Bill of Rights. Important segments of Federalist opinion continued to regard a bill of rights as unnecessary, and were concerned that any amendments would weaken the new government. South Carolina's first Senators, Ralph Izard and Pierce Butler, were staunch Federalists, and neither harbored much enthusiasm for a bill of rights. Izard captured this sentiment when he wrote to Thomas Jefferson: "I hope we shall not be wasting time with idle discussions about amendments to the Constitution, but that we shall go to work immediately about the finances. . . . "[122]

During the Senate debate he sought to postpone consideration of the suggested constitutional amendments. In August of 1789 Butler belittled the significance of the amendments then under discussion. "A few milk-and-water amendments," he observed, "have been proposed by Mr. M[adison], such as liberty of conscience, a free press, and one or two general things already well secured."[123]

William L. Smith, who was elected to represent Charleston District in the House of Representatives, was similarly disinclined to push for a declaration of rights. He twice sought to delay debate until the federal government was organized.[124] Smith's role in drafting the proposed amendments was very limited. He even objected to the phrase prohibiting "cruel and unusual punishments" on the ground it was "too indefinite."[125]

South Carolina's other Representatives, however, were more receptive to constitutional amendments. In the first Congressional canvass critics of the Constitution were elected in three of the state's five districts.[126] Indeed, Representatives Aedanus Burke and Thomas Sumter had voted against ratification at the South Carolina convention. Hence, the election results underscored the continuing strength of Antifederalist views among the general population, and placed opposition leaders in a strong position to promote a bill of rights.

As might be expected, Burke, Sumter and Representative Thomas Tucker hoped to reduce federal authority in relation to the states. They favored more extensive amendments than those proposed by James Madison and the select committee to compose a bill of rights. Although Burke served as a member of the special committee, he was displeased with the report and declared:

> . . . I am very well satisfied that those that are reported and likely to be adopted by the House are very far from giving satisfaction to our constituents; they are not those solid and substantial amendments which the people expect; they are little better than whip-syllabub, frothy and full of wind, formed only to please the palate; or they are like a tub thrown out to a whale, to secure the freight of the ship and its peaceful voyage.[127]

Accordingly, Burke, Sumter and Tucker unsuccessfully supported a series of resolutions to weaken the power of the federal government, or to enhance popular rights. Tucker, for example, moved to insert the right of the people to instruct their representatives how to vote on pending issues.[128] He also attempted to add the word "expressly" to the language of what became the 10th Amendment.[129] This proposal, if adopted, would have strengthened the states by curtailing the doctrine of implied powers. As recommended by the South Carolina convention, Tucker sought to prevent the levy of a direct tax until Congress had attempted a requisition of the states.[130] Burke proposed an amendment to curtail the maintenance of a standing army in time of peace.[131]

In short, all segments of the South Carolina delegation shared a lack of enthusiasm about the Bill of Rights. The Federalists did not actively obstruct a declaration of rights, but they assigned it a low priority and wished to concentrate upon other matters. Antifederalists, on the other hand, were unhappy with the narrow scope of the proposed changes. Burke, Sumter and Tucker even voted against the conference committee report which adopted the Senate wording on two amendments.[132]

Ratification of the Bill of Rights by the South Carolina legislature was expeditious and uneventful. On January 7, 1790 Governor Charles Pinckney formally reported that Congress had submitted a series of constitutional amendments to the states.[133] The congressional resolution was referred to a House committee, which reported on January 18. While conducting a variety of other business, the House on that day approved all twelve of the original proposed amendments. The vote was apparently unanimous.[134] In addition, the House "instructed" South Carolina's Congressional delegation "to propose the amendments recommended by the Convention of this State" for adoption as part of the Constitution. Lastly, the House rejected a move by the New York legislature to convene another convention in order to revise the Constitution.[135] The Senate promptly concurred in the House's action.

Thus, South Carolina ratified the Bill of Rights in a casual, almost offhand manner. Judging from surviving newspaper accounts of the brief legislative session, the Bill of Rights created no public stir and was not a source of controversy.[136] Indeed, the press was preoccupied with complaints about the inconvenience of meeting for the first time in Columbia and the plans for a state census.[137] Although it is always difficult to evaluate negative evidence, the absence of debate suggests that lawmakers understood that the Bill of Rights would simply confirm the existing rights of the citizens and states.

IV

Following South Carolina's ratification vote the Charleston newspapers carried a cartoon which pictured the state as the eighth pillar in the temple of the United States. The story of how the Palmetto State became the eighth pillar is perhaps not as dramatic as the bitter and close ratification struggles elsewhere. Yet the South Carolina contest tells us much about the sectional divisions within the state and the socio-economic interests which pushed for ratification. It also foreshadows the political changes that would occur when the conservative low country elite could no longer control South Carolina.

# Constitutional Silences: Georgia, the Constitution, and the Bill of Rights—A Historical Test of Originalism

PETER CHARLES HOFFER

In these years of heavily publicized controversy over appointments to the United States Supreme Court, an historical essay on Georgia's ratification of the federal Constitution may seem tame antiquarianism. In fact, the larger historical context of her acceptance of the federal system, stretching through the momentous test of will in *Chisholm v. Georgia,* has much to tell us about the current debate over constitutional originalism. A short summary of the latter will serve as an introduction to the Georgia tale, which in turn teaches a lesson for modern jurists.

The Senate hearings on the appointment of Robert Bork to the United States Supreme Court in the Fall of 1987 carried the issue of constitutional originalism from the pages of the law journals[1] and the rostrums of bar meetings and placed it squarely before the public.[2] Bork had argued that the constitution ought to be narrowly construed, according to its letter, measured against the ascertainable purposes of its authors.[3] He joined (at least before the hearings on his confirmation began) with Chief Justice William Rehnquist, Attorney General Edwin Meese, and Assistant Attorney General William Bradford Reynolds,[4] and a cohort of friendly academics, in rejecting the notion of a living constitution.[5] There is some confusion whether originalism requires discovery and application of the personal intentions of the framers, or allows a broader reading of their general purposes.[6] However modified, originalism rejects the proposition that the plain sense of the words may change over time as they are read in new contexts, or that judges have a positive duty to bring the language of the Constitution up to date.

Arrayed against this formidable authority is a phalanx of liberal jurists and legal scholars, led by United States Supreme Court Justice William Brennan and Harvard Law School professor Lawrence Tribe. The core of the constitutional jurisprudence of these liberals is that the document invites periodic reexamination; that the framers themselves intended such periodic reinterpretation; that the principles of constitutional construction entail sensitivity to the current meaning of terms; and that policy and public welfare require that literalism bow to present needs.[7]

For law scholars, jurists, and now the public at large vicariously present in the Senate confirmation hearings, the subject is one of great moment. Invariably, if not necessarily, originalism is a conservative doctrine.[8] The principles and objectives of the framers, as novel and liberal (both politically and economically) as they were for the end of the 18th century,[9] are entirely out of step with our current policies on minority rights, welfare state planning, civil liberties, and democratic pluralism. Conservatives have argued that earlier Supreme Courts' non-originalist activism on behalf of big business against organized labor, Populist and Progressive state regulatory activity, and private reform organizations in the "Lochner Era"[10] demonstrates, even for the most naively trusting liberals, the evils that flow from activist courts inventing law to assist special groups. Liberals have retorted that the restraint or activism of the courts is not dictated by originalism or its rejection, but by a wholly different sort of consideration—the judges' view of the role of the courts in our government.[11]

For the jurists and law professors in this debate, history is a solid, apparently fixed source of inspiration and evidence. The historian considering the roots of our constitutionalism will view the function of history in the debate from a different perspective.

The law scholar takes the historical record as a given; the working historian knows how tenuous the written evidence is, how filled with gaps, silences, and deliberate falsifications. As James Hutson has recently demonstrated,[12] many of the first-hand accounts of the Constitutional Convention and the ratifying conventions upon which legal scholars and jurists rely must be used with extreme caution.[13] The recovery of the framers' personal motives and broad purposes is rarely easy and never irrebuttable.[14] The effect that the uncertainty of historical research might have upon legal argument was apparent at a recent conference in Cambridge, Massachusetts.[15] Joyce Appleby, an early modern intellectual historian, asked Charles Fried, a Harvard Professor of Law on leave as Solicitor General, what would happen to his own originalist interpretation of the Constitution if new documents happened to turn up to show that key framers wanted an open-textured document, capable of great expansion in future, and understood their product to have been just that. The solicitor general was at a loss for an answer. Recent work on some of the framers has pointed toward this conclusion, as it happens, though that work is still in its early stages.[16]

The record of Georgia's response to the Constitution and the Bill of Rights presents the historian's dilemma, and with it, the trap for the unwary legal scholar, in its starkest form. Georgians were appointed to the Convention and sat with it, for varying times, from the first meetings to the closing session. Georgia ratified the Constitution in the winter of 1788, without dissent. Georgia did not ratify the Bill of Rights until 150 years after it went into effect. The record, which we will review in a moment, is filled with silences. Yet Georgia was responsible, again through silent (or near silent) resistance, for the first major test of the manner in which the Constitution was to be construed in the courts, and the first major formal alteration in its text. Georgia's relative silence leading up to *Chisholm v. Georgia*[17] presents a challenge for the historian, and a lesson for the law scholar.

The Georgia Assembly (its only legislative body under the

Constitution of 1777) named six delegates to the Convention in Philadelphia.[18] George Walton and Nathaniel Pendleton, representing two of the many factions in that state's tumultuously partisan political universe, never went. William Pierce, a perennially unsuccessful artisan, merchant, and entrepreneur, William Few, a South Carolina immigrant who succeeded as a planter and politician from one of the most influential families in the state, and Abraham Baldwin, a transplanted Connecticut educator, lawyer, and former minister, did attend the convention.[19] Pierce left after a month, William Houstoun stayed only briefly, but Few and Baldwin sat punctually, and both signed for Georgia.[20] Pierce[21] and Baldwin,[22] at different times, contributed to the fashioning of the "Great Compromise" over representation in the upper house. Pierce's character sketches of the delegates to the convention[23] demonstrate his common sense and keen appreciation of physical appearance and oratorical skills—a source for cultural history that has not yet been utilized.[24] It is not very useful on constitutional history, unfortunately.

Pierce carried the document back to Augusta, then the capital of the state, and presented it to the legislature, which authorized election of a ratifying convention.[25] The Georgia *Gazette*, Augusta's only newspaper, had prepared the way for the convention, publishing brief pieces on the need for reform of the confederation,[26] and on the eve of the Georgia ratifying convention, reprinting James Wilson's Federalist address to the Pennsylvania ratifying convention. The paper offered the speech to its readers to "convince those lukewarm geniuses, who hesitate adopting the Constitution, lest they be robbed of all their consequence, pride, and ambition."[27] From the 28th of December to the 2nd of January, the state convention met, debated and ratified the federal document.[28] Unlike many of the other states, the Georgians proposed no amendments. Georgians neither discussed nor ratified the Bill of Rights.

That is, in essence, the extent of the historical record. What is the historian to do with this silence?

Were we concerned with the silence as solely a problem of historical sources, that is, without commenting on the use of history by constitutional scholars, we might conclude with a few paragraphs of measured speculation on the reasons for Georgia's conduct. In the light of the use and abuse made of our earliest constitutional history in the debate over originalism, this course would constitute a dereliction of public duty. The feasibility of originalism in the face of silence (a far wider topic than is immediately apparent, for much of the current debate concerns the interstices, the silences, of the Constitution), is a question that historians of our Constitution should face directly.

To be sure, the silence of primary sources is one of the technical problems historians encounter, and surmount, in the normal course of our work. Every historian of early Georgia faces this difficulty. Much of the colonial record was destroyed in the battle for Savannah during the Revolutionary War. In the early statehood period, there were few printing presses, newspapers, and other means of dissemination of information. Her population was scattered across a vast and insecure frontier, over whose edges coursed Indians and Spanish colonists hostile to her existence. Although she was no longer the focus of imperial contest, she was never safe from local uprisings, often caused by her own settlers' lust for Indian lands. Neither Savannah nor Augusta, her two largest towns, were centers of culture. The former was a busy port, the latter an up-river mart, but neither had a college (though chartered in 1785, the University of Georgia was not open to students until 1801, and did not thrive until a generation later), or a coterie of intellectuals. Her politics were a rough and tumble mixture of personal allegiances, personal affronts, and partisan scraps over land, debt, and patronage.

What did the advent of a federal Constitution mean to judges, legislators and executive officers in such a place? In all likelihood, it meant, first and foremost, security from outside attack. Notices of the progress of the delegates in Philadelphia were all but crowded off the pages of the *Gazette* by alarms and reports of

Indians raids. News of treaty negotiations with the Creeks alternated with preparations for war against them.[29] The *Gazette* also carried a full report on the rebellion in Western Massachusetts, a salutary warning of the danger of domestic insurrection.[30] The newspaper also chronicled the fragile peace in Europe, its readers knowing full well how eruption of war among European powers spilled over the ocean and into the forests of the New World.[31] Throughout the Indian wars, Georgia's neighbors had rendered her little or no assistance. A stronger central government could guard the seacoast and the frontier, in a way in which individual states could not.[32] Close students of Georgia's early history agree that protection from invasion was of prime importance to Georgia's leaders. In this context, the Guarantee Clause of the federal Constitution was less an invitation to the federal government to intervene in local affairs,[33] than it was a promise that the federal government would come to the aid of a state beset by outside agitators and filibusterers, Indians, and foreign powers.

Collateral historical evidence reveals a second strand of Georgia's attachment to the new Constitution. In 1789, the state undertook to revise its own constitution. Her original constitution was, with Pennsylvania's, the most populist in structure, giving power of appointment and the purse to a unicameral legislature. Conservatives, including William Houstoun, feared that property was never safe from the whim of the mob under the old form of state government. In one of his infrequent contributions in Philadelphia he looked ahead to the revision of the state constitution.[34] Two years later, his expectations were fulfilled. Following the example of South Carolina and Pennsylvania, also in the midst of the "second wave" of state constitution-making, Georgians decided to revise their constitution. The resulting document strongly resembled the federal constitution.[35] In the constitution of 1789, the unicameral legislature disappeared. A single executive was created, though he was still chosen by the legislative branch (the method advocated in the Virginia Plan proposed in Philadelphia Convention, and the way in which Virginia Governors were named). A senate was established, whose electees were to hold office for three times as long as the assemblymen. The judiciary was made more independent of the other branches. Without doubt the new federal government served as the structural model for revision in Georgia. The state's framers' debt to the federal framers was great. The federal separation of powers was a product of over a century of theorizing and experimenting with checks and balances—the division of power among different functional organs of government, protecting the government from capture by a single faction, while insuring access to government for many factions. Georgians did not have to repeat this long and arduous process of elucidation—they had only to duplicate its end result.

Taken together, the unanimity and dispatch of ratification, and the imitation of the federal structure in Georgia suggest that most leading elements in the state wanted the imposition of more order in their affairs. William Few recalled that none of the delegates was entirely happy with the Constitution when they left Philadelphia, but it was the best compromise they could obtain.[36] The tenor of his recollections, penned in 1816, may be taken as an indicator of his neighbors' response. For Georgia, exposed to external threats and internal dissention, a federal government was a necessity.

At the same time as Georgians welcomed federal protection and structural models, the state's leaders assumed that certain areas of governance were exclusively the state's concern, and they read this assumption into the silences of the Constitution. This doctrine of enumerated powers, sanctified in the litany of the Tenth Amendment, made its appearance early and often in the Constitutional Convention. From the first debates over the scope of Congress's powers, the delegates confronted the desirability of constitutional silence. One of these debates vitally interested the ordinarily quiet Georgia delegation. On the 22nd of August, 1787, a small band of New England and Middle Atlantic delegates resumed their attack upon the international slave trade.[37] When these delegates proposed that the Constitution bar the importation of slaves, the South Carolina delegation rose as one and threatened to bolt if the state's importation of slaves was curtailed.[38] Oliver Ellsworth of Connecticut tried to mediate the dispute, suggesting that the Constitution be silent on the question, as the natural progress of the nation's economy, and the growth of her free labor supply, would eventually antiquate the institution of slavery.[39] Abraham Baldwin entered the debate to insist that slavery was a local concern, a domestic institution best regulated by state law. Baldwin hinted that the state might well end the trade, though he condemned the extremism of certain sects (undoubtedly referring to the Quakers and the Mennonites) who demanded equality for all persons.[40] Baldwin was either too innocent or too cunning in these surmises. Georgia was wedded to the slave system, as Betty Wood's recent book incontrovertibly demonstrates.[41] Whether Baldwin was embarrassed defending his state's vital interests in the presence of his old compatriots from Connecticut (particularly Ellsworth, who had gone out of his way to state that *he* had never owned a slave) or meant to pacify his new constituents, cannot be determined. The record is silent on that question.

We have now fully ventured into the world of historical silences, that is, where the historical record does not mandate a conclusion, though context and external evidence may strongly suggest it. Even proceeding in this self-denying manner, we can suggest two larger conclusions about Georgia's constitutionalism. First, for a frontier state like Georgia, the federal government was a protector, rather than an alternative or even a co-ordinate system of governance. Nothing in her reliance upon federal assistance against invasion or insurrection, or the borrowing of federal models for internal constitutional reform, implied that Georgia had yielded its sovereignty, its control over its own domestic affairs.

Georgia's ratifiers understood that a dual sovereignty had been erected, in which federal law was supreme (according to Article VI, section 2 of the Constitution) in those areas where federal authority was stipulated. How could the provisions of Article III, section 2, on the jurisdiction of the Supreme Court, be read differently from other explicit enumerations of federal power?

Clashes between a state and the federal government over tariffs, the war making power, coinage, the creation of new states, the making of treaties, and the creation of inferior federal tribunals, to name a few areas of these enumerated powers, were to be resolved by the federal government. To this Georgia had acceded. Or had it?

Seen in this light, Georgia's silence raises complex constitutional questions. When a legislature, a drafting convention, or a ratifying convention refuses to address an issue or a contingency in its final written product, that silence can be a source of great controversy. Our courts generally refuse to fill silences in statutes or constitutional provisions with positive commands, but there are noteworthy exceptions. [42] The response of the court is often predicated upon the full historical context of the silence (including the alternative wordings of the statute raised and discarded in the legislative debate). The origin of these constitutional silences lie at the heart of the historian's quarrel with originalism. [43] How does one maintain originalism when the voices of the framers—and with them, the plain meaning of the originators' text—are silent. Is every common-law innovation, spurred by social improvement or economic necessity, to be rejected because the judge cannot recover the drafters' intent? Must new legislation be drafted before the courts can respond to changing realities, that is, give remedies for real damages? Must the limitations of the framers' human vision automatically become limitations on later courts? If the general case of this conundrum is primarily the concern of jurists and law professors, legal historians know that courts never have surrendered their power to do justice in the face of legislative silence. As Guido Calabresi had recently reminded us, courts are wont to use subterfuges, legal fictions, or even tricks to update obsolete statutes, emend obscure constitutional provisions, and extend the generalities of the Constitution to new kinds of claims. [44] It is the courts' job to adjudicate cases; they are functional, not theoretical, institutions. Whether in public law litigation, where entire classes of litigants are pitted against entire municipalities, counties, or states, or in a dispute over run-off from a downspout between neighbors, the courts cannot remain silent, they must adjudicate the suit and give reasons for their decision. Even dismissal of the suit for want of standing, that is, failure of the suitor to show that she is entitled to the ear of the court, is voiced rather than silent.[45]

In the Georgia case, the historian can begin to penetrate these silences by expanding the context of ratification to include Georgia's conduct in *Chisholm*. We must assume that Georgians understood the Constitution to reduce their own state's sovereignty; the question for them was the limit of that intrusion.[46] Their truculent silence in *Chisholm* was originalism with a vengeance, as we will see.[47]

The facts in *Chisholm* were simple and reflected a problem common after the Revolutionary War. The state had contracted to pay Robert Farquhar of South Carolina for supplies during the conflict, but had not fulfilled its promise. The testator of the contractee, Alexander Chisholm, could not get satisfaction in the circuit federal court,[48] which had jurisdiction over the case under section 25 of the Judiciary Act of 1789.[49] Judge James Iredell dismissed for want of jurisdiction in the case.[50] Chisholm could have turned to the state court in Georgia, but elected instead to take the case to the United States Supreme Court, which had concurrent jurisdiction over claims between citizens of one state and another state, under Article III, section 2 of the Constitution, and the above section of the Judiciary Act. The high court agreed to hear the case in 1792, but Georgia refused to obey the summons to appear. The court postponed the case until its February 1793 session, to give the state a second chance to come to court. Georgia allowed its counsel, Jared Ingersoll and Alexander Dallas (both leading attorneys at the Philadelphia bar, and the latter the reporter of the Supreme Court) to read a statement into the record objecting to the jurisdiction of the court, but the state refused to participate further in the cause, and by implication, appeared to resist the authority of the court.[51] Here was the first genuine challenge to the supremacy clause of the Constitution,[52] the authority of the Supreme Court, and the legislative power of the Congress.[53]

All of the justices agreed that the case was an important one, though the damages for the breach could hardly have been earth-shattering. The issues themselves made the suit one of "uncommon magnitude."[54] Virginia's Edmund Randolph, attorney general of the United States, represented the plaintiff in his capacity as a private attorney, not then regarded as a breach of professional ethics. The irony in this case was that Randolph, in the course of his brief, had to speak as conservator of federal jurisdiction as well as counsel for his client. He admitted as much when he said that the suit was unpopular in his own state as well as Georgia, but it would be "official perfidy" to ignore the constitutional question.[55]

Randolph's framing of the argument for Chisholm provided the basis for almost all of the justices' opinions. He divided his client's case into four questions: (a) could the state of Georgia be sued in federal court, notwithstanding its sovereignty, and if so, by a citizen of another state; (b) if Georgia could be a defendant in federal court, would the action of assumpsit lie against it;[56] (c) was service of the papers upon the governor and attorney general of the state sufficient; and (d) by what process ought the decision of the federal courts be enforced against a state?

His answer to the first question began with the plain text of the Constitution and the Judiciary Act of 1789. Though "human genius" (that is, the ingenuity of counsel) might read the constitutional provision for suits between "states and citizens of another state" to mean that a state could be a plaintiff, the Supreme Court's jurisdiction in suits by one state against another meant that states could be defendants as well.[57] This may seem a variety of originalism, but Randolph did not rest with the letter of the law, much less its authors' intent. Although he was one of the framers, he probed the spirit of the law, that is, its larger purpose. He did not ask what the personal motivations of the framers might be, but looked to the context of their collective endeavor, the rationale for the new government. One of the evils of the confederation was that a plaintiff had no neutral forum when he brought suit against a state not his own. The framers knew that courts and legislatures in states were human, vulnerable to partisan passions.[58] The federal Constitution produced a "new order of things," whose purpose was greater than the sum of the framers' individual aims. An "easy and usual construction" of the text of the Constitution ought to convince the Supreme Court that federal jurisdiction infringed upon the pre-constitutional sovereignty of all the states, even though all the justices knew that many of the delegates feared such centralized courts.[59]

The architecture of Randolph's argument seems modern, or at least relevant to the modern debate over originalism, and the reader should consider the significance of the similarity. Randolph had witnessed the creation of the new government, but he did not rest his case upon intimate personal knowledge of intent. Instead, he asked what were the broad purposes of the new government. Again, in a manner that post-realist[60] scholars ought to applaud, Randolph gave weight to the policy considerations of the framers. "Public harmony" could not withstand a state court's refusing justice to an out-of-state litigant. The result would be the very war of each against all which the federal government was instituted to prevent.[61] For the federal union to survive, states must submit themselves as parties in federal court. Randolph's vision of the future of constitutional discourse failed but once in his treatment of the first question, when he resisted the idea that the federal government could be sued, in the same way that a state could be sued.[62]

Randolph disposed of the final three questions in short compass. He found justification for an action of assumpsit in the general rule of common law that where there is a right, there must be a remedy.[63] The state had made a promise, and it was, after all, no more than an assemblage of people. If they, as individuals would be liable, so would the state.[64] The action of assumpsit was designed for this breach, and was in use in almost all common-law courts. On the third issue, the competency of service, Randolph noted that the governor of Georgia was currently suing a citizen of South Carolina for a debt owed Georgia. If the governor was competent to bring suit for the state, he was competent to be served the papers as a defendant when the state was sued.[65] The final question, of enforcement, was potentially the most difficult. It would actuate Justice Iredell's exhaustive, convoluted, and tenacious dissent from the majority of the court. Randolph preferred to dismiss it with the pious hope that Georgia would obey the court.[66]

It is surely dangerous for the historian to regard Randolph as a direct forerunner of the non-originalists, save in the respect that Randolph knew well that he and his successors would have to stretch the language of the Constitution to cover situations the founders had not anticipated, or preferred not to contemplate. As the attorney general adopted a non-originalist position, the first justice to render an opinion (in the era before John Marshall, justices on the Supreme Court, like judges of the high courts in England, read their own opinion on every case) adopted a style of Constitutional reasoning that anticipated Robert Bork's. James Iredell of North Carolina knew that Georgia was already mounting a campaign in Congress to amend the Constitution to avert an unfavorable ruling in *Chisholm*.[67] For two weeks, the court deliberated the case, no doubt listening to Iredell's dire warnings of potential disobedience. No court wants to render a decision it knows will be disregarded, or that it cannot enforce.[68] Iredell could not convince his brethren, and wrote at length to justify his foreboding. It would be unfair to him to regard his opinion as a brief for the defense, though his advocacy verged upon that extreme. As such, it was far closer to style of opinions written by modern appellate judges, than the far more terse and dispassionate opinions of the judges of his own era.[69]

He admitted that the case was a "great cause" and had no precedent.[70] In the vacuum of settled law, Iredell refused to act as a common law judge, that is, to reason by analogy. Relying upon his ruling on circuit, he asserted that if the letter of the Constitution and the Judiciary Acts did not mention the action of assumpsit, it could not be brought. [71] The Supreme Court, in his opinion, had no authority to construe the Constitution or the Judiciary Acts to provide remedies where they were not explicitly allowed. It was the duty of the Congress to legislate, "it is *ours* only to *judge* [italics in original]." [72] Iredell laid the foundation for future claims of judicial restraint in language that Judge Bork might well adopt: "There is no part of the constitution that I know of, that authorizes this court to take up any business where they left it, and order that the powers given in the constitution may be in full activity, supply their omission by making *new laws* for *new cases*; or which I take to be the same thing, applying *old principles* to *new cases* materially different from those to which they were applied before [italics in original]." [73]

Iredell did have to distinguish assumpsit from the other "principles and usages of law" [74] which were to govern process in the federal courts. Randolph had assumed that assumpsit could be deduced from this blanket authorization. To hurdle this obstacle, Iredell proposed that common usage meant literally that—the usages of all the states. Georgia did not allow assumpsit against itself, hence that action, that is, assumpsit against a state, could not be part of the common usages and principles available to the federal courts. [75] An originalist faced with the text of the Judiciary act, but determined to resist it for other reasons (which could not be justified under the formal rules of originalism) must attempt something like this with the text. By linking assumpsit, which Georgia did allow in her own courts, with suits against the state, not permitted in Georgia, Iredell prevented Georgia's allowance of assumpsit in private litigation from being used as a precedent against her. Of course, the end result is a circular argument, assuming the truth of the very proposition Georgia had to establish to avert a suit against itself. The problem for the defendant was, of course, that the letter of the Constitution allowed just such a suit against a state, and gave jurisdiction in such a suit to the circuit court or the Supreme Court. Iredell must have recognized that this argument was not wholly persuasive, but it was the sort of very close reasoning that was left him in the face of his election to argue from the text, rather than from broad principles or policy.

He was on firmer ground when he objected to violation of the principle of sovereign immunity. He could employ precedent to good effect. A review of English cases and authorities sufficed to establish that a private citizen could not sue the crown but by petition (that is, in effect, with the permission of the crown). There was thus no compulsory remedy against the crown. Nor, he averred, was there a remedy against a sovereign state, even when the state defaulted upon its debts.[76] Debts could be collected from corporations, because these were mere collective organizations (the very characterization of states Randolph offered), but Iredell rejected the premise that states were chartered creatures of the federal government. The justice parried Randolph's thrust by analogy. If states were mere collections of individuals (Randolph's argument), and corporations were mere collections of individuals (the standard view of corporations until the last three decades of the nineteenth century[77]) then states could have no more legal rights than corporations. Iredell found this untenable, given that the states antedated the federal government and retained considerable immunity from federal intrusion under the Constitution.[78] The states represented the sovereignty of the people of the state. Such sovereign bodies must not be dishonored by compulsory attendance in the circuit courts at the suit of a private citizen of another state.[79]

Iredell had fought long and hard in North Carolina for ratification of the Constitution. He did not wish to undermine its authority, or demean his public support for it, in *Chisholm*. In a tortured closing sentence he tried to except his opposition to federal jurisdiction in the case at hand while upholding the supremacy of federal law: "This opinion, I hold, however, with all the reserve proper for one, which according to my sentiments in this case, may be deemed in some measure extra-judicial."[80] Iredell's warning was unmistakable: it was bad policy, a word he belatedly introduced in his final remarks, for the high court to insist upon this jurisdiction. "I pray to God," he concluded, "that if the attorney-general's doctrine, as to the law, be established by the judgment of this court, all the good he predicts from it may take place, and none of the evils with which, I have the concern to say, it appears to me to be pregnant."[81]

Justice James Blair of Virginia, speaking next, found the case important but easy. "When a state, by adopting the constitution, has agreed to be amenable to the judicial power of the United States, she has, in that respect, given up her right of sovereignty."[82] Georgia herself relied upon federal jurisdiction to collect a debt from Brailsford. At the same time, Blair agreed with Iredell that a judgment for recovery by default might be too precipitate; Georgia ought to be given a third chance to appear in court to argue its case.[83]

Justice James Wilson took a more philosophical approach to the dispute than Iredell or Blair. To him it was a matter not only of law, but of natural justice. Citing Scottish common-sense moral philosopher Thomas Reid, Wilson, who had emigrated from Scotland as a young man, warned against pernicious mischief done in the name of state sovereignty. The state was an "inferior contrivance"[84] subordinate to the will and needs of the people. "As the state has claimed precedence of the people; so, in the same inverted course of things, the government has often claimed precedence of the state; and to this perversion in the second degree, many of the volumes of confusion concerning sovereignty owe their existence."[85] The state was an "artificial person" with rights and obligations, including those owed to private individuals to whom it had, in its official capacity, pledged its trust. Such a body "ought" to do justice and fulfill obligations.[86] Could a dishonest state, like a dishonest merchant, willfully refuse to honor its commitments, then shield itself behind a cloak of sovereign immunity? Wilson concluded "Surely not."[87] Wilson's rhetoric obscured the fact that Georgia's state government undoubtedly represented the will of its people in resisting federal suits against the public treasury by out-of-state creditors. By arguing that a state's willful refusal to submit itself to suit was a relic of a feudal tyranny[88] (in a compressed and somewhat inaccurate summary of the development of sovereign immunity), Wilson misread what the state of Georgia thought it was doing. By comparing Georgia's posture to King George III's, Wilson reached for a political, even a propaganda, advantage, in what he must have decided would be a highly publicized decision. Much of his opinion must be read in that light, though at its end, he returned to the central constitutional issue: The "people of the United States intended to bind the several states, by the legislative power of the national government."[89] Without this common obedience, there could be no tranquility, uniform justice, or clarity of law. Though the "most consummate degree of professional ingenuity"[90] (surely a reference to Iredell's opinion) might argue that a state could not be a defendant in a federal court, the language of the federal Constitution and the Judiciary Acts was plain. The action lay against Georgia. Wilson was silent on the question of enforcement, a pregnant silence, given Georgia's public expression of resistance.[91]

For Justice William Cushing of Massachusetts, the issues were as simple as they were for Blair. The judicial power was "expressly" extended to cases like *Chisholm*, and states could clearly be defendants in federal courts.[92] The policy behind this apportionment of judicial authority was obvious: the states could not carry out the great designs of the federal government, one of which was the equal protection ("the claim to justice equal") of all citizens, wherever they might bring just claims.[93] Cushing did not flinch from the logical conclusion that the United States must also be suable in its own courts, though he saw no need to pursue the issue in the present case.[94]

John Jay, as Chief Justice the last to speak, turned back to the Revolutionary War for his text. The people then considered themselves a nation. When the experiment with confederation failed, they created a general government. The preamble to the Constitution established the great purposes of the new government, reminding Americans that government rested upon the sovereignty of the people. Governments, he agreed with Wilson, were mere collectives, obliged to do justice to persons who had claims against them. The "equal liberty" of a South Carolina citizen to obtain justice against Georgia rested upon these simple, sturdy foundations. Georgia was not privileged to ignore the legal claims of those who had contracted with it; to allow that would make non-Georgia citizens inferior to Georgia citizens, insofar as Georgia was obligated to honor its commitments to the latter. [95]

Jay was also concerned that Georgia's refusal to honor its legal obligations to citizens of other states would extend to debts it owed foreigners. One of the reasons he had so strongly supported the federalist movement was his realization that only a strong national government would induce Europeans to enter into treaties with the United States. [96] The price of that respectability was the supremacy of treaties over local law authorized by Article III, section 2, and Article VI, section 2. If Georgia could resist the common-law claims of South Carolinians, she could ignore those of British claimants raised under provisions of the Peace Treaty of 1783. British nationals suing for their pre-war debts and the return of property confiscated during war had made little headway in state courts. By assuring these suitors a fair trial in federal court, the new Constitution made the United States far more legitimate in foreign eyes. If Georgia could bar suits against itself by other Americans, how might she regard suits by her ex-enemies, whose armies had ravaged her coasts and burned her settlements? There was plenty of evidence from other states that British claims would be resisted. [97] For aliens, then, as well of citizens of other states, the recourse to federal courts in suits against states was "useful, because it is honest, because it leaves not even the most obscure and friendless citizen without means of obtaining justice from a neighboring state; because it obviates occasions of quarrels between states on account of the claims of their respective citizens; because it recognizes and strongly rests on this great moral truth, that justice is the same whether due from one man to a million, or from a million to one man; because it teaches and greatly appreciates the value of our free republican national government . . . "[98] Jay, like Wilson, knew that his words would reach far beyond the court, and closed with political rhetoric. After all, with Wilson, he had been one of the architects of the ratification of the Constitution, and had a stake in its continued vitality.

If Chisholm won the battle, Georgia won the war. While the Court waited for Georgia to respond to its summons, Georgia delegates led the Congress to a swift and crushing defeat of the Court. The Eleventh Amendment eliminated federal jurisdiction over suits between one state and citizens of another state.[99] If Georgia's silence in *Chisholm* was fraudulent, part of her determination to resist the decision by any means rather than submit to the rule of law, a position belatedly vindicated when other states' Congressmen and Senators joined in voting for the amendment, what does this say about her view of the Constitution? Was her swift and unanimous ratification hypocrisy? Or was it part of a genuine confusion over the uses to which federal courts would be put?

Blair, Wilson and Randolph all noted that Georgia herself came into the Supreme Court to sue in *Georgia v. Brailsford*.[100] The state had confiscated property belonging to a Tory during the war, but out-of-state defendants held a legal interest in it. Could they collect, or was the property now Georgia's to dispose of as it chose. For the plaintiff-state, Ingersoll and Dallas argued that the wartime confiscation acts were just that, a dispossession. For the defendants, William Bradford, who had replaced Randolph as attorney general, but had the brief as a private counsel, argued that the Georgia confiscation statute only created a constructive trust, sequestering the property for the duration of the war.[101] Chief Justice Jay instructed a jury on the court's view of the law: the Georgia act was no more than a sequestration. The jury was left to find the facts: were the debts due to the state, or to the defendants. They found the latter.[102]

Before we condemn Georgia to the part of Hell reserved for constitutional perfidy, we must recognize that Georgia was not alone in wanting all the benefits and none of the liabilities of the new Union. The "vehement speed"[103] with which the Eleventh Amendment was proposed and passed is one indication of the support for Georgia's views, but not the first evidence of it. New Hampshire had ratified the Constitution but urged that diversity suits (between citizens of different states) begin in the courts of the respective states, and be appealable to federal courts only when the damages sought exceeded $3,000.[104] Virginia's proposed amendments even more severely limited federal court jurisdiction.[105] New York's ratifiers would have forbidden any suit in federal courts against a state.[106] They lost, but the losers in the federal system can always reopen a cause through revised construction of the Constitution or, failing that, amendment. Georgia played by the letter of these rules, if not entirely in their spirit.

Georgia did not ratify the Bill of Rights. There is no evidence in her legislative records that the matter was ever debated.[107] She had guarantees of rights in her constitution, including freedom of religion, press, assembly, and the right to jury trial,[108] but these rights were not gathered into a formal declaration preceding or following the body of the constitution.[109] Georgia played no role in the drafting of the Bill of Rights, though James Gunn, one of her senators, did attempt to add a guarantee of jury trial in all criminal cases.[110] He failed in this, and the rest of the record is silence until 1941, when Georgia ratified the Bill of Rights as a "token gesture."[111]

Georgia was not alone in her refusal to ratify; she was joined by Massachusetts and Connecticut, the only two states whose religious establishments persisted into the nineteenth century. There may be some irony in this continuation of the Baldwin-Ellsworth connection, but its larger significance need not concern us.

What is the lesson for the originalist in this historical discourse? Most simply, it may be to leave history to the historians. If valid, this conclusion is parochial and condescending to our sister discipline of law. Better is the recognition that Iredell's literalism was unable to convince his brethren because it did not come to grips with the reality of the case before them. He might have engaged them in the debate over the broad principles of the Constitution. He hinted at the policy that underlay his dissent in his final paragraphs. Then he veered away from policy, in the fashion of an originalist. True, the modern originalist would have to concede federal jurisdiction in the case, but Iredell's failure, and theirs, is a deeper one, a failure to penetrate beneath the formulas of law to its social essence, to come to grips with social reality behind the claims and defenses of the parties. This is what Wilson and Jay attempted to do, albeit in the language of late eighteenth century republicanism which they had done so much to elucidate. Georgia's silence, like Iredell's technical special pleading, was originalist. She could not come to court because her leaders could not formulate a realistic alternative to federal jurisdiction in suits like *Chisholm*. They could not fall back upon the letter of the Constitution, and so embraced the originalist's only alternative— amendment. It may thus be ironic that out of Georgia's constitutional silence came the one great victory for originalism in our constitutional history—the Eleventh Amendment.

Even that victory has proven pyrrhic. The reach of the Amendment was soon curtailed in a series of decisions by John Marshall, allowing suit against state officials, in their own name, and federal suits against states when the state itself had commenced the suit in its own courts. Though the doctrine was reinvigorated in the gilded age, it has again gone into eclipse in our own time.[112] The Amendment thus stands as one more evidence of the way in which our courts fill historical silences with constitutional meaning according to the needs and demands of modern life.

# Notes

Notes to INTRODUCTION

1. Charles Sackett Sydnor, "The Southerner and the Laws," *Journal of Southern History* 6 (1940):2–23.

2. Kermit L. Hall and James W. Ely, Jr., "The South and the Constitution," in Hall and Ely, eds., *An Uncertain Tradition: Constitutionalism and the History of the South* (Athens: University of Georgia Press, 1988), 3–16.

3. Jack P. Greene, "The Constitution of 1787 and the Question of Southern Distinctiveness," p. 21 of this volume.

4. Edward C. Papenfuse, "The 'Amending Fathers' and the Constitution: Changing Perceptions of Home Rule and Who Should Rule at Home," p. 74 of this volume.

5. Peter C. Hoffer, "Constitutional Silences: Georgia, the Constitution, and the Bill of Rights—An Historical Test of Originalism," p. 134 of this volume.


Notes to THE CONSTITUTION OF 1787 AND THE QUESTION OF SOUTHERN DISTINCTIVENESS
*by Jack P. Greene*

1. As quoted by John Richard Alden, *The First South* (Baton Rouge: Louisiana State University Press, 1961), p. 17.

2. [John Fothergill], *Considerations Relative to the North American Colonies* (London: H. Kent, 1765), pp. 36–43.

3. Benjamin Rush's Notes for a Speech in Congress, [Aug. 1, 1776], in Paul H. Smith, et al., eds., *Letter of Delegates to Congress* (Washington, D.C.: Library of Congress, 1976–), 4: 592, 599.

4. John Adams to Joseph Hawley, 25 November 1775, ibid., 2:385.

5. Joseph Galloway to [Samuel Verplanck], 30 December 1774, ibid., 1:288.

6. Adams to Hawley, 25 November 1775, ibid., 2:385–86.

7. "John Dickinson's Notes for a Speech in Congress," July 1, 1776, ibid., 4:356.

8. Hamilton, *Federalist* #13, in Jacob E. Cooke, ed., *The Federalist* (Middletown: Wesleyan University Press, 1961), p. 80.

9. See Jack P. Greene, *Pursuits of Happiness: The Social Development of Early Modern British Colonies and the Formation of American Culture* (Chapel Hill: University of North Carolina Press, 1988), and Carl Bridenbaugh, *Myths and Realities: Societies of the Colonial South* (Baton Rouge: Louisiana State University Press, 1952).

10. H. James Henderson, *Party Politics in the Continental Congress* (New York: McGraw-Hill, 1974). See also Joseph L. Davis, *Sectionalism in American Politics, 1774–1787* (Madison: University of Wisconsin Press, 1977).

11. As quoted by Alden, *First South*, p. 51.

12. Adrienne Koch, ed., *Notes on Debates in the Federal Convention of 1787 Reported by James Madison* (Athens: Ohio University Press, 1966), p. 84 (Gerry); p. 133 (Hamilton); p. 550 (Madison).

13. Ibid., p. 216 (Hamilton); Jonathan Elliot, ed., *The Debates in the Several State Ratifying Conventions on the Adoption of the Federal Constitution*, 4 vols., (New York: B. Franklin, 1968 [1836]), 3:278, 616 (Grayson); 3:312–13 (Madison).

14. Koch, *Notes of Debates*, p. 124 (Patterson); p. 429 (Mason); Elliot, *Debates*, 3:615 (Grayson).

15. Koch, *Notes of Debates*, p. 270 (Rutledge).

16. Ibid., pp. 224–25 (Madison).

17. Ibid., p. 285 (G. Morris).

18. Ibid., p. 232 (Charles Pinckney); p. 261 (King and Dayton); p. 467 (Mason).

19. Ibid., p. 269 (Mason).

20. Ibid., p. 295 (Madison).

21. Ibid.

22. Ibid., p. 261 (Dayton).

23. Ibid., p. 261 (C. C. Pinckney).

24. Elliot, *Debates*, 4:296–97 (Barnwell); 3:633 (Innes); 4:151 (Maclaine).

25. Ibid., 4:135 (Bloodworth).

26. Ibid., 186 (Iredell).

27. Ibid., 323–24 (Charles Pinckney).

28. John Jay to Granville Sharp, 1788, in Henry P. Jackson, ed., *The Correspondence and Public Papers of John Jay* (New York: 1890–93), 3:342, as quoted by William W. Freehling, "The Founding Fathers and Slavery," *American Historical Review,* 77 (1972): 86.

29. Arthur Zilversmit, *The First Emancipation: The Abolition of Slavery in the North* (Chicago: University of Chicago Press, 1967); Donald L. Robinson, *Slavery in the Structure of American Politics 1765–1820* (New York: Harcourt, Brace & Jovanovich, 1971).

30. Koch, *Notes of Debates*, p. 502 (Martin).

31. Ibid., p. 411 (G. Morris).

32. Ibid., pp. 503–04 (Mason).

33. Ibid., p. 502 (Rutledge); p. 505 (Charles Pinckney and C. C. Pinckney).

34. Lachlan McIntosh to John Wereat, 17 December 1787, in Merrill Jensen et al., eds., *The Documentary History of the Ratification of the Constitution* (Madison: Wisconsin State Historical Society, 1978–), 3:260–61.

35. Elliot, *Debates*, 4:272–73 (Lowndes).

36. Ibid., 3:590–91 (Henry); 3:270 (Mason).

37. Ibid., 453 (Madison).

38. Ibid., 285–86 (C. C. Pinckney).

39. Ibid., 598–99 (Randolph).

40. David M. Potter, "The Historians' Use of Nationalism and Vice Versa," *American Historical Review,* 68 (1962): 935, 949.

41. Elliot, *Debates*, 4:100–01 (Galloway and Iredell).

42. Alden, *First South*, pp. 90–98; Calvin C. Jillson and Cecil L. Eubanks, "The Political Structure of Constitution Making: The Federal Constitution of 1787," *American Journal of Political Science,* 27 (1984): 452.

43. Forrest McDonald, *We the People: The Economic Origins of the Constitution* (Chicago: University of Chicago Press, 1958), p. 96.

44. Jillson and Eubanks, "Political Structure of Constitution Making," 439–47.

45. As quoted by Alden, *First South*, pp. 9–10.

46. Elliot, *Debates*, 3:615 (Grayson); 113 (Corbin). See also the article by Drew McCoy, "James Madison and Visions of American Nationality in the Confederation Period: A Regional Perspective," in *Beyond Confederation: Origins of the Constitution and American National Identity*, ed. by Richard Beeman, Stephen Botein and Edward C. Carter, II (Chapel Hill: University of North Carolina Press, 1987), pp. 234–36.

47. Daniel P. Jordan, *Political Leadership in Jefferson's Virginia* (Charlottesville: University Press of Virginia, 1983); Norman K. Risjord, *The Old Republicans: Southern Conservatism in the Age of Jefferson* (New York: Columbia University Press, 1985).

48. The data on exports and population may be found in *Historical Statistics of the United States, Colonial Times to 1980* (Washington: Government Printing Office, 1975), Part 2, pp. 1168–78.

49. Elliott, *Debates*, 4:276–77 (Rutledge); 335 (C. C. Pinckney); 124 (M'Dowall); 186 (Iredell); Koch, *Notes of Debates*, p. 286 (Butler); 274 (Madison); Alden, *First South*, pp. 105–06.

50. Koch, *Notes of Debates*, p. 161 (Sherman).

51. Elliot, *Debates*, 4:285 (C. C. Pinckney).

52. Koch, *Notes of Debates*, p. 505 (C. C. Pinckney).

53. Elliot, *Debates*, 3:314 (Henry); 277 (Grayson).

54. Joyce Appleby, "What is Still American in the Political Philosophy of Thomas Jefferson?," *William and Mary Quarterly*, 3d ser., 34 (1982): 292.

55. Risjord, *Old Republicans*.

56. Potter, "Historians' Use of Nationalism," 943; C. Vann Woodward, "The Southern Ethic in a Puritan World," *William & Mary Quarterly*, 3d ser., 25 (1968): 343–70.

57. Joseph F. Kett and Patricia A. McClung, "Book Culture in Post-Revolutionary Virginia," *American Antiquarian Society Proceedings*, 94 (1984), Pt. 1:136. Robert E. Shalhope, "Thomas Jefferson's Republicanism and Antebellum Southern Thought," *Journal of Southern History*, 42 (1976): 529–56. The Washington quotation is from Yehoshua Arieli, *Individualism and Nationalism in American Ideology* (Cambridge: Harvard University Press, 1964), p. 27.

Notes to NATURAL RIGHTS, BILLS OF RIGHTS, AND THE PEOPLE'S RIGHTS IN VIRGINIA CONSTITUTIONAL DISCOURSE, 1787–1791
*by David Thomas Konig*

1. David J. Bodenhamer and James W. Ely, Jr., eds., *Ambivalent Legacy: A Legal History of the South* (Jackson: University Press of Mississippi, 1984), which sets out this theme in the editors' introductory essay, "Regionalism and the Legal History of the South," pp. 3–29.

2. Mason's remark was related by Hugh Williamson to John Gray Blount, 3 June 1788, in Edmund Cody Burnett, *Letters of Members of the Continental Congress* 8 vols. (Washington: Carnegie Institution, 1921–36), 8:747.

3. Madison to George Washington, 18 October 1787, in Gaillard Hunt, ed., *The Writings of James Madison* 9 vols. (New York: G. P. Putnam's, 1900–1910), 5: 12.

4. Madison to Archibald Stuart, 30 October 1787, ibid., p. 47.

5. Carrington to William Short, 25 October 1787, in Burnett, *Letters of Members of Congress*, 8: 665.

6. Carrington to James Madison, 23 September 1787, ibid., 647.

7. Jonathan Elliot, ed., *The Debates in the Several State Conventions, on the Adoption of the Federal Constitution, as Recommended by the General Convention at Philadelphia, in 1787* 4 vols. (New York: B. Franklin, 1968 [1836]), 3:138.

8. Mason to Martin Cockburn, 1 December 1788, in Robert A. Rutland, ed., *The George Mason Papers 1725–1792* 3 vols. paged consecutively (Chapel Hill: University of North Carolina Press, 1970), 1136.

9. Elliot, *Debates*, 3:561.

10. Francis N. Thorpe, comp., *The Federal and State Constitutions, Colonial Charters, and Other Organic Laws of the States, Territories, and Colonies Now or Heretofore Forming the United States of America* 7 vols. (Washington: Government Printing Office, 1909), 7: 3812–3814. (Emphasis added.)

11. On this distinction, and on the nature of precatory constitutional language, see Robert C. Palmer, "Liberties as Constitutional Provisions," in William E. Nelson and Robert C. Palmer, eds., *Liberty and Community: Constitution and Rights in the Early American Republic* (New York: Oceana, 1987). The present paper is much indebted to this insightful piece.

12. Compare Mason's language in the Virginia Bill of Rights—and that in every other new state bill of rights, for that matter—with that in the English Bill of Rights, in W. C. Costin and J. Steven Watson, eds., *The Law and Working of the Constitution: Documents 1660–1914* 2 vols. (London: A. & C. Black, 1952), 2: 67–74.

13. Elliot, *Debates*, 3: 66–67 (Randolph), 140 (Henry).

14. For example, see Edward Dumbauld, *Thomas Jefferson and the Law* (Norman: University of Oklahoma Press, 1978), pp. 85–87.

15. Jefferson used chapter iii of Book VI of Samuel Pufendorf, *De Jure Naturae et Gentium* in *Howell v. Netherland* (1770), while Richard Bland used that same chapter (albeit a different section) two years later in in *Robin v. Hardaway*. Interestingly, Bland's opposing counsel in that case, none other than George Mason, relied on this same chapter (citing yet other, different sections of the chapter) to oppose slavery. Mason won this case, but Jefferson could not follow his argument, so "Contradictory" was it. On these cases, see Dumbauld, *Jefferson and the Law*, pp. 214–215n.

16. Stanley N. Katz, "Thomas Jefferson and the Right to Property in Revolutionary America," *Journal of Law and Economics* 19 (1976): 467–488.

17. Julian P. Boyd, *et al.*, eds., *The Papers of Thomas Jefferson* (Princeton: Princeton University Press, 1950–), 2: 546–547.

18. St. George Tucker, sitting on Virginia's highest court in 1806, would explain away the dilemma by holding that the natural law statement regarding freedom and the equality of all men in the Declaration of Independence "was meant to embrace the case of free citizens, or aliens, only; and not by a side wind to overturn the rights of property." *Hudgins v. Wright*, 11 Va 133, 140. On the federal Supreme Court, Chief Justice John Marshall in 1825 confessed that slavery was contrary to natural law, but sanctioned by international law. *The Antelope*, 10 Wheaton, 66.

19. Max Farrand, ed., *The Records of the Federal Convention of 1787* 4 vols. (New Haven: Yale University Press, 1911–37), 2: 417.

20. Elliot, *Debates*, 3: 621–622.

21. "Cato Uticensis," 17 October 1787, in Herbert J. Storing, ed., *The Complete Antifederalist* 7 vols. (Chicago: University of Chicago Press, 1981), 5: 123.

22. Madison to George Washington, 4 June 1788, in Merrill Jensen, ed., *Documentary History of the Ratification of the Constitution* (Madison: Wisconsin State Historical Society, 1978–), 4: 683.

23. Elliot, *Debates*, 3: 186.

24. Ibid., 620. On the English antecedents, see Wallace Notestein, *et al.*, eds., *Commons Debates 1621* 6 vols. (New Haven: Yale University Press, 1935), 6: 332–336.

25. "Denatus," in the *Virginia Independent Chronicle*, 11 June 1788, in Storing, *Complete Antifederalist*, 5: 260–267.

26. Elliot, *Debates*, 3: 657–661.

27. Mason is cited by Robert A. Rutland, *The Ordeal of the Constitution: The Antifederalists and the Ratification Struggle*. 1787–1788 (Norman: University of Oklahoma Press, 1966), p. 14. Randolph's remark appears in Elliot, *Debates*, 3: 25.

28. For Madison, see Joseph Gales, comp., *Annals of the Congress of the United States . . .* , I: March 3, 1789 to March 3, 1791 (Washington: Gales and Seaton, 1834), 448. For Mason, see *Notes of Debates in the Federal Convention of 1787 Reported by James Madison* (Athens: Ohio University Press, 1966), p. 630.

29. Jacob E. Cooke, ed., *The Federalist* (Middletown: Wesleyan University Press, 1961), 386 (Number 57, for "communion"), 361 (Number 53, for "paramount").

30. David Thomas Konig, "Country Justice: The Rural Roots of Constitutionalism in Prerevolutionary Virginia," in *An Uncertain Tradition: Constitutionalism and the History of the South*, ed. by Kermit L. Hall and James W. Ely, Jr. (Athens: University of Georgia Press, 1989), 63–82. On another state's aversion to writing down such rules, see Walter F. Pratt, Jr., "Oral and Written Cultures: North Carolina and the Constitution, 1787–1791," in the present volume.

31. Elliot, *Debates*, 3: 30.

32. Rutland, *Papers of Mason*, 895–898.

33. Elliot, *Debates*, 3: 540, 579. See also the same point made by William Grayson, *ibid.*, 274, 566.

34. Boyd, *Papers of Jefferson*, 6: 286.

35. See, especially, the "Remonstrance" by members of the Virginia Court of Appeals against being injected into this struggle, and against assuming such a burden without any additional pay, reprinted in David J. Mays, ed., *The Papers of Edmund Pendleton 1734–1803* 2 vols. paged consecutively (Charlottesville: University Press of Virginia, 1967), 505–509.

36. Pendleton to James Madison, 19 December 1786, in Mays, *Papers of Pendleton*, p. 490.

37. Madison to James Monroe, 30 December 1785, in Hunt, *Writings of Madison*, 2: 211.

38. Madison to Caleb Wallace, 13 August 1785, ibid., 171.

39. *Annals of Congress*, 1: 451.

40. Ibid., 452.

41. Ibid., 458.


Notes to THE "AMENDING FATHERS" AND THE CONSTITUTION: CHANGING PERCEPTIONS OF HOME RULE AND WHO SHOULD RULE AT HOME
by Edward C. Papenfuse


1. Richard Hofstadter, *The Idea of a Party System The Rise of Legitimate Opposition in the United States, 1780–1840* (Berkeley: University of California Press, 1972), Chapters 1, 2, and p. 13.

2. A. E. Dick Howard, *The Road from Runnymede Magna Carta and Constitutionalism in America* (Charlottesville, Va: University Press of Virginia, 1968.

Thomas Jefferson to Dr. Walter Jones, January 2, 1814, reprinted by Herman S. Frey, Frey Enterprises, 605 Merritt Street, Nashville, TN 37203, n.d., as "Thomas Jefferson's Description of George Washington."

3. For an excellent overview of the constitution making process in the states see: Willi Paul Adams, *The First American Constitutions Republican Ideology and the Making of the State Constitutions in the Revolutionary Era* (Chapel Hill: University of North Carolina Press, 1980). Professor A. E. Dick Howard in *The Road from Runnymede Magna Carta and Constitutionalism in America* (Charlottesville: The University Press of Virginia, 1968), traces the English origins of the American state constitutions back to the Magna Carta. See also Edward C. Papenfuse, "Magna Carta," in the Baltimore *Sun*, September 2, 1987. Possibly no single document was as well known by name to the Founding Fathers than the Magna which the Barons forced King John to accept on June 15, 1215. It was a "bill of rights" that formed and integral part of the English legal heritage universally accepted by the thirteen original colonies. Yet when the Constitutional Convention met in Philadelphia in the summer of 1787, the document it produced lacked any hint it was not needed given the universally accepted traditions of the English Constitution and the constitutions of the individual states. Others, including an active minority in Maryland led by a signer of the Declaration of Independence, William Paca, felt otherwise.

Maryland's State Constitution, adopted in 1776, already contained a Declaration of Rights, among which was the provision "That no freeman ought to be taken, or imprisoned, or disseized of his freehold, liberties, or privileges, or outlawed, or exiled, or in any manner destroyed, or deprived of his life, liberty, or property, but by the judgment of his peers, or by the law of the land."

In 1215 the Barons imposed upon King John their own Bill of Rights, among which was the provision that "No Free man shall be taken, imprisoned, disseised, outlawed, banished, or in any way destroyed, nor will we proceed against or prosecute him, except by the lawful judgment of his equals or by the law of the land." So strong was the influence of the Magna Carta with regard to the importance of the rule of law that in 1776, 561 years after Magna Carta, those who wrote Maryland's first State Constitution would in part make Magna Carta's language their own.

In April of 1788, just as workmen were completing the exterior of the magnificent wooden dome atop the present Maryland State House, the Maryland Ratifying Convention assembled in the old House of Delegate's chamber. Twelve members of the Maryland Ratifying Convention did their best to convince the majority to consider 28 amendments, among which was one that would make it unconstitutional to in any way "repeal or abrogate the constitutions or bills or rights of the states or any part of them."

Indeed, when explaining why they had argued for a specific amendment restraining the application of martial law except in time of war (ultimately incorporated into the 5th amendment to the U. S. Constitution), the minority wrote: "This provision . . . although, by no means so ample as that provided by magna charta, and the other fundamental and constitutional laws of Great Britain, (it being contrary to magna Carta to punish a freeman by martial law in time of peace,) . . . yet it may prove an inestimable check, for all other provisions in favour of the rights of men would be vain and nugatory, if the power of subjecting all men to bear arms to martial law at any moment should remain vested in congress."

Although the Maryland effort to amend the Constitution proved unsuccessful in the Maryland Ratifying Convention of April 1788, the widely circulated printed report of the minority, the first such printed agenda for a Bill of Rights, had a profound influence on the remaining States that had not yet ratified. Within the first year of the new government the first Amendments to the U. S. Constitution collectively known as the Bill of Rights were on their way back to the states for approval containing language that derived in part from what the Barons forced King John to affix his seal of approval in 1215.

4. For a detailed discussion of the changing role of state government in the lives of the governed and its impact on local politics, see: Edward C. Papenfuse, "The Legislative Response to a Costly War: Fiscal Policy and Factional Politics in Maryland 1777–1789," in Ronald Hoffman and Peter J. Albert, eds., *Sovereign States in an Age of Uncertainty* (Charlottesville: Published for the United States Capitol Historical Society by the University Press of Virginia, 1981), pp. 134–156. It takes national issues and the writing of a national constitution to fundamentally alter the character of local politics.

5. *Maryland Gazette and Baltimore Advertiser,* September 14, 1787.

6. From the Report of the Annapolis Convention signed by the Chairman John Dickinson and as reported in *The New-Jersey Gazette,* Monday, October 2, 1786.

7. H. A. Washington, *The Writings of Thomas Jefferson* (Washington: Taylor & Maury, 1853), pp. 52, 58.

8. Broadside printed by the *Maryland Gazette and Baltimore Advertiser.* The *Maryland Journal* (Baltimore), published the text of the Constitution on September 25. The *Maryland Gazette* (Annapolis) followed on September 27.

9. Little attention has been paid to Tench Coxe's articles as the *American Citizen* as a concerted effort on the part of the pro-Constitution forces to enlist former loyalists. Although the importance of the nonjurors to the consensus on the Constitution sought by the Federalists cannot be addressed in detail here, virtually nothing has been written on the subject. A chronology of the appearance and distribution of the essays by *An American Citizen* is:

1787, Sept 26  First essay dated in *American Museum,* II 301–06
1787, Sept 27  Coxe wrote Madison enclosing essay(s)? (1–3?)
1787, Sept 28  Second essay dated in *American Museum,* II, 4th essay undated, pp. 387–91
1787, Sept 29  Third essay dated in *American Museum,* II, 4th essay undated, pp. 387–91
1787, Oct 1  Madison writes Coxe commending him
1787, Oct 5  First essay published in *Maryland Gazette* (Balt)
1787, Oct 9  Second essay published in *Maryland Gazette* (Balt)
1787, Oct 12  Third essay published in *Maryland Gazette* (Balt)
1787, Oct 16  Madison tells Coxe he has given essays to Hamilton
1787, Oct 21  Wrote Madison enclosing? other essay? (#4?)
1787, Oct 23  Sends all four essays to William Tilghman
1787, Oct 24  All? reprinted in *Pennsylvania Gazette*
1787, Nov 2  Fourth Essay published in Maryland Gazette (Balt)
1787, Nov 3  Madison tells Coxe essays published as a pamphlet in Virginia (1–3); no. 4 in the newspaper.

The thrust of Coxe's argument is that the proposed Constitution is even better than the British Constitution. The proposed Constitution is safe from ecclesiastical tyranny. There will be no placemen, no rotten boroughs. Coxe is decidedly anti-slave trade, if not slavery. He argues that the new government will not impinge upon state governments, there will be no ex post facto laws, and elections will be regulated by each of the states. He concludes that a bill of rights is not needed and has a long section on trial by jury.

10. John Francis Mercer deserves closer attention as an opponent of the Constitu-

tion. He had no difficulty being accepted into the Maryland ruling elite when he moved to Maryland from Virginia and married well, yet he proved to be a leading exponent of the expanded franchise and supporter of debtors like Charles Ridgely against their British creditors.

11. Forrest and Jefferson are quoted by Peter S. Onuf, *The Origins of the Federal Republican: Jurisdictional Controversies in the United States, 1775–1787* (Philadelphia: University of Pennsylvania Press, 1983), p. 175. For Forrest's biography see Edward C. Papenfuse, Alan F. Day, David W. Jordan, and Gregory A. Stiverson, *A Biographical Dictionary of the Maryland Legislature 1635–1789* (Baltimore: The Johns Hopkins University Press, 1979), I: 324–325.

12. Edward C. Papenfuse, "The Legislative Response to a Costly War Fiscal Policy and Factional Politics in Maryland 1777–1789," in Ronald Hoffman and Peter J. Albert, eds., *Sovereign States in an Age of Uncertainty* (Charlottesville: University Press of Virginia, 1981), pp. 134–156. A different view of Chesapeake politics is to be found in Jackson Turner Main, *Political Parties Before the Constitution* (New York: W. W. Norton & Co., 1974), pp. 212–243, and Norman K. Risjord, *Chesapeake Politics 1781–1800* (New York: Columbia University Press, 1978). See Edward C. Papenfuse's review of *Chesapeake Politics* in the *Maryland Historian*, Fall 1979 issue in which Risjord's model of political behavior in the Chesapeake Bay region is questioned in greater detail.

13. Edward Gaylord Bourne, ed., *The Federalist* (New York: Tudor Publishing Co., 1937), pp. 62–70.

14. Thomas Stone letter quoted by Dorothy S. Eaton and Vincent L. Eaton, in "The Dye is Cast . . . ," *Library of Congress Quarterly Journal of Current Acquisitions* 14 (1957):181–185.

15. Willi Paul Adams, *The First American Constitutions* (Chapel Hill: University of North Carolina Press, 1980).

16. [Annapolis] *Maryland Gazette*, July 18, 1776.

17. Edward Papenfuse and Gregory Stiverson, *Decisive Blow is Struck* (Annapolis: Maryland Hall of Records, 1977), pp. 5 and 1 ff. For a brief discussion of the 'troubled spring of 1776' see: Peter Charles Hoffer, " 'Their Trustees and Servants': Eighteenth-Century Maryland Lawyers and the Constitutional Implications of Equity Precepts," *Maryland Historical Magazine* 82 (Summer 1987):142–143.

18. *The Decisive Blow is Struck*, p. 21.

19. Thornton Anderson, "Maryland's Property Qualifications for Office: A Reinterpretation of the Constitutional Convention of 1776," *Maryland Historical Magazine*, 73 (December, 1978): 327–339, and Anderson, "Eighteenth-Century Suffrage: The Case of Maryland," ibid., 76 (June, 1981): 141–158.

20. *Carlisle [Pennsylvania] Gazette*, February 27 and March 19, 1788.

21. *Maryland Historical Magazine*, 83 (Spring 1988), pp. 18–35. See also an expanded version in Patrick T. Conley and John P. Kaminski, *The Constitution and the States: The Role of the Original Thirteen in the Framing and Adoption of the Federal Constitution* (Madison, Wisconsin: Madison House, 1988), pp. 133–154.

22. *Pennsylvania Packet*, May 2, 1788.

23. Draft in William Paca's hand, Maryland State Archives, Special Collection MdHR 1592.

24. *Journal of Public Law*, 7 (1958): pp. 323–344.

25. Ibid., and "Richard Henry Lee's Proposed Amendments, 27 September" in *The Documentary History of the Ratification of the Constitution*, Merrill Jensen, ed., (Madison: State Historical Society of Wisconsin), 1:337–339.

26. The original drafts of the amendments offered at the Maryland Ratification

Convention in April 1788 are in Maryland State Archives Special Collections, MdHR G 1592. For a discussion of the Maryland Amendments see Gregory A. Stiverson, "Maryland's Antifederalists and the Perfection of the U. S. Constitution," *Maryland Historical Magazine* 83 (Spring 1988): 18–35.

27. For the text of the Declaration of Rights and amendments proposed by Virginia see: *Documents Illustrative of the Formation of the Union of the American States* (Washington: Government Printing Office, 1927), pp. 1027–1034.

28. Adult white males over 21 with 50 acres of land or L30 common currency (current money) could vote. In 1782 the population was estimated at 35,268 white males over 18, but this cannot account for soldiers still in the army. Anderson (*Maryland Historical Magazine*, Vol. 73–4: n. 19) suggests 4.5% reduction to give realistic estimate of those over 21: 33,680.94. He then estimates that 63.8% of the Free Adult males had enough property to vote suggesting that about 21,488 could vote in 1782 and 21,738 in 1783 (Anderson *Maryland Historical Magazine*, Vol. 76–2:150). Anderson qualifies this further with some discussion of free blacks, reducing % to 62, but his conclusion remains basically unaltered: the result is "a figure not irreconcilable with the estimate of 25,000 in 1788 cited above." He derives the 25,000 from Crowl who cites a 1788 article in the *Maryland Journal*. Based upon Thorton's calculations, 12.5893% of the total white population was eligible to vote (possibly lower in Baltimore City where there were more people who had less then L30 of property?) Thornton indicates that in Baltimore County, 58% of the Free Adult White Males were eligible to vote (*Maryland Historical Magazine*, Vol. 76–2:149). The best estimate of the population of Baltimore about 1790 (Greene and Harrington: 133) was 12,248 whites. My calculations for 1783, based upon the tax lists is: 9,597 whites, up from an estimated total population of 6,000 in 1776 (Merrill Jensen, *The New Nation*, 115). Assuming the lower eligibility rate for Baltimore city (10.458% of the total white population), then the voting population in 1776 was less than 627, when adjusted for slaves in the total population. In 1783 it was 1004, and in 1790, 1280. We know however, that in 1788, 1342 people voted in BC, so it probably makes more sense to use the state-wide figure offered by Anderson of .125893 of the total population which would make 1776 less than 755, 1783 about 1208, and 1790, 1542.

29. Based upon an analysis of returns and population. See Philip A. Crowl, *Maryland During and After the Revolution A Political and Economic Study* (Baltimore: The Johns Hopkins University Press, 1943), pp. 165–168.

30. For discussions of the nature of the Maryland political and economic elite see: Robert Forster and Edward C. Papenfuse, "Grands planteurs du Maryland au XVIII siecle," *Annales*, 37 (May–June 1982):552–573 and "Gerer un Patrimoine dans les deux Mondes: les Carrol d'Annapolis (Maryland) et les Dupont de la Rochelle (1750–1830)," *Annuario Dell'Istituto Storico Italiano per L'Eta Moderna E Contemporanea*, 33–34 (1981–1982): 9–23.

31. *Maryland Gazette and Baltimore Advertiser*, October 5, 1787. The best discussion of the elections in Baltimore City in 1787 and 1788, as well as an overview of the whole period is to be found in William Arthur O'Brien, "Challenge to Consensus: Social, Political and Economic Implications of Maryland Sectionalism, 1776–1789," unpublished Ph.D. dissertation, University of Wisconsin-Madison, 1979. O'Brien tries to make the section model of Main and Risjord work without any great success, but his coverage of the sources and degree of detail is commendable.

32. In 1802 the law was changed to vote by ballot, a decided plus for party activity. It was not until 1890 that the 'Belgian' or secret ballot was adopted in Maryland. See

Bernard Christian Steiner, *The Institutions and Civil Government of Maryland* (Boston: The Athenaeum Press, 1899), pp. 195–195. Steiner prefers the term 'Belgian' ballot to 'Australian' because the Belgian ballot arranges all the candidates for one party together and the Australian ballot does not.

33. For a discussion of Hammond and the factions in the Constitutional Convention of 1776, see: Papenfuse and Stiverson, *The Decisive Blow is Struck*, unpaginated introduction.

34. See the essays in *"Anywhere So Long As There Be Freedom" Charles Carroll of Carrollton, His Family & His Maryland*, edited by Ann C. Van Devanter (Baltimore: The Baltimore Museum of Art, 1975), especially those by Sally Mason, Ronald Hoffman, and Edward C. Papenfuse.

35. In addition to O'Brien's work, *op. cit.*, see also James Haw, Francis F. Bierne, Rosamund R. Bierne, and R. Samuel Jett, *Stormy Patriot The Life of Samuel Chase* (Baltimore: Maryland Historical Society, 1980) for the elections in Baltimore City and Chase's career.

36. Ibid.

37. See Charles G. Steffen, *The Mechanics of Baltimore: Workers and Politics in the Age of Revolution, 1763–1812* (Urbana: University of Illinois Press, 1984).

38. Edward C. Papenfuse, "An Undelivered Defense of a Winning Cause: Charles Carroll of Carrollton's 'Remarks on the Proposed Federal Constitution,'" *Maryland Historical Magazine*, 71 (Spring 1976): 220–251.

39. William Tilghman to Tench Coxe, 4 February 1787, Historical Society of Pennsylvania, Microfilm edition of the Coxe Papers, reel 1008.

40. *Votes and Proceedings of the House of Delegates, November 1789*, pp. 33, 39: "[November 23, 1789] Mr. W. Tilghman, from the committee, brings in and delivers to Mr. Speaker a bill, entitled of, the constitution of the articles in addition to, and amendment of, the constitution of the United States of America, . . ." "[November 24, 1789] The bill to ratify certain articles in addition to, and amendment of, the constitution of the United States of America, proposed by congress to the legislatures of the several states, was read the second time, passed, and sent to the senate by Mr. W. Tilghman."

41. *Charleston [South Carolina] Morning Post & City Gazette*, January 21, 1790.

42. For the Black List controversy see Crowl, *Maryland During and After the Revolution* and O'Brien "Challenge to Conservatism."

43. [John Francis Mercer], essay on the removal of the seat of government to Baltimore, [1816].

44. Ronald Hoffman, *A Spirit of Dissension Economics, Politics, and the Resolution in Maryland* (Baltimore: The Johns Hopkins University Press, 1973).


Notes to ORAL AND WRITTEN CULTURES: NORTH CAROLINA AND THE CONSTITUTION, 1787–1791
*by Walter F. Pratt, Jr.*


1. "In the Convention the North Carolina delegation was comparatively mediocre rather than distinguished in ability and reputation. In the framing of the Constitution it played a creditable and important though not leading or conspicuous role; but it did not represent faithfully the views and wishes of agrarian, radical, provincial North Carolina," Albert Newsome, "North Carolina's Ratification of the Federal Constitution," *North Carolina Historical Review* 17 (1940): 288.

Allan Nevins, *The American States During and After the Revolution, 1775–1789* (New York: Macmillan, 1924), p. 406.

2. Jonathan Elliot, ed., *Debates in the Several State Conventions on the Adoption of the Constitution,* 5 vols. (Philadelphia: J. B. Lippincott, 1888), 4:242.; Augustus W. Clason, *Seven Conventions* (New York: D. Appleton, 1888), p. 120. North Carolina was no stranger to ambivalent approvals. In 1776, when the provincial congress attempted to draft a constitution for the state, the delegates were unable to agree; they postponed the debate for six months. See "Samuel Johnston and Thomas Jones to James Iredell, May, 1776" in William Saunders, ed., *Colonial Records of North Carolina,* 26 vols. (Raleigh: P. M. Hale, 1890), 10:1037–38; Samuel A. Ashe, *History of North Carolina,* 2 vols. (Greensboro: Van Noppell, 1908), 1:527–31, 556–69; Hugh Lefler & William Powell, *Colonial North Carolina* (New York: Scribners, 1973), pp. 281–83; Henry M. Wagstaff, *State Rights and Political Parties in North Carolina, 1776–1861,* Johns Hopkins University Studies in Historical and Political Science, ser. 24, nos. 7–8 (Baltimore: Johns Hopkins University Press, 1906), pp. 9–12. Some years later, when the Articles of Confederation came before the state legislature, a joint legislative committee recommended approval of only those parts of the Articles of Confederation "immediately essential to the success of the present war." Full approval should come only after "full time and leisure for maturely and deliberately considering" the remaining articles. Merrill Jensen, ed., *The Documentary History of the Ratification of the Constitution: Constitutional Documents and Records, 1776–1787* (Madison: Wisconsin State Historical Society, 1978–), 1:124; Walter Clark, ed., *The State Records of North Carolina,* 26 vols. (Raleigh: P. M. Hale, 1902), 12:229. Four months later the legislature adopted the Articles in full. *Documentary History History of Ratification,* 1:125–126; Merrill Jensen, *The Articles of Confederation: An Interpretation of the Social-Constitutional History of the American Revolution* (Madison: University of Wisconsin Press, 1940), p. 186

3. North Carolina's first convention voted against ratification on August 2, 1788. According to the Moravian records, a number of people began to change their opinions almost immediately. Adelaide Fries, ed., *Records of the Moravians in North Carolina,* 9 vols. (Raleigh: Edwards & Broughton, 1922–1941), 5:2223. William Hooper informed his brother that "the temper of the Western country has taken an entire change with respect to the new constitution . . . ." See [William Hooper] to his brother, 23 October 1788, William Hooper Papers, North Carolina State Archives [NCSA], Raleigh, North Carolina. On October 2, 1789, President George Washington transmitted the proposed amendments to Governor Samuel Johnston of North Carolina. Washington to Samuel Johnston, October 2, 1789, (photocopy), Governors' Papers, No. 17, NCSA.

The second convention ratified the Constitution on November 21, 1789, by a vote of 195–77. *North Carolina State Records,* 22:48–49. Louise Trenholme noted that only 194 names are listed as voting for the Constitution. Louise Trenholme, *The Ratification of the Federal Constitution in North Carolina* (New York: Columbia University Press, 1932), p. 238 n.25. The Federalists were unable to secure the convention's ratification of the amendments proposed by Congress. The convention did, however, propose eight amendments of its own. *North Carolina State Records,* 22:51–52. Nevertheless, a month later, on December 22, 1789, the state's legislature approved the Bill of Rights. For a chronology of that final step in joining the union see Newsome, "North Carolina's Ratification," p. 300 n. 14.

4. Newsome, "North Carolina's Ratification," p. 301 n. 15.

5. The first two southern states to hold conventions, Delaware (December 7,

1787) and Georgia (December 31, 1787), voted unanimously in favor of the Constitution. The next two had overwhelming majorities in favor of the Constitution: Maryland, 63–11 (April 26, 1788) and South Carolina, 149–73 (May 23, 1788). Only in the critical state of Virginia was the vote close, 89–79 (June 25, 1788). See Jensen, *Documentary History of the Ratification of the Constitution*, 1:22–23.

6. Willi Paul Adams has noted the absence of "resistance" or "amazement" that the first state constitutions were written. Willi P. Adams, *The First American Constitutions: Republican Ideology and the Making of the State Constitutions in the Revolutionary Era* (Chapel Hill: University of North Carolina Press, 1980), p. 22. But as he also notes, the first "constitutions" were little more than ordinary law. Moreover, they represented no effort by a group outside the states to impose control. In other words, these first state constitutions lacked the full *written* character that emerged in the federal constitution as discussed below. Fletcher Green also commented on the written character of the first state constitutions, but without analyzing the importance of the characteristic. Fletcher M. Green, *Constitutional Development in the South Atlantic States, 1776–1860* (Chapel Hill: University of North Carolina Press, 1930), pp. 51–52. See also Thomas Bender, *Community and Social Change in America* (New Brunswick: Rutgers University Press, 1982), p. 84 for a discussion of the emergent national political culture as "contractual in the modern sense and rel[ying] upon precise articulation of rights and duties—in writing, as in the case of the Bill of Rights."

7. See generally Kenneth A. Lockridge, *Literacy in Colonial New England: An Enquiry into the Social Context of Literacy in the Early Modern West* (New York: Norton, 1974). Deborah Tannen made a similar point in summarizing scholarship on orality and literacy. She noted "that literate tradition does not replace oral. Rather, when literacy is introduced, the two are superimposed upon and intertwined with each other." Deborah Tannen, "The Oral/Literate Continuum in Discourse," in Tannen, ed., *Spoken and Written Language: Exploring Orality and Literacy* (Norwood, N. J.: ABLEX Corp., 1982), p. 3.

8. Cf. Bender, *Community and Social Change*, p. 84; Daniel H. Calhoun, *The Intelligence of A People* (Princeton: Princeton University Press, 1973), p. 38; Brian Street, *Literacy in Theory and Practice* (Cambridge: Cambridge University Press, 1984), pp. 45–6; Robert H. Wiebe, *The Segmented Society: An Introduction to the Meaning of America* (New York: Alfred Knopf, 1975), pp. 15–16; Rhys Isaac, "Books and the Social Authority of Learning: The Case of Mid-Eighteenth-Century Virginia," in William L. Joyce, et. al., eds., *Printing and Society in Early America* (Worcester: American Antiquarian Society, 1983), pp. 243–44.

9. See Adams, *First American Constitutions*, pp. 29–30.

10. For example, during the ratification debate in North Carolina, William R. Davie said that the "radical vice" of the Confederation was that its legislation acted on states rather than on individuals. Elliot, *Debates*, 4:21–22.

11. "The constitutional resolution of 1789 combined two political cultures, one formal and contractual, the other essentially communal. . . . [The national elite who drafted the Constitution] spoke for a 'Great Tradition' of politics that was somewhat detached from local communities, and the political structure they created, reflecting this tradition, was liberal rather than communal. It envisioned a politics of conflicting interests that would be moderated by a translocal political elite. This was an innovation for Americans used to a politics that was, as with the ancient Greeks, fundamentally face-to-face and local." Thomas Bender, *Community and Social Change*, p. 83. Cf. Eric A. Havelock, *Preface to Plato* (Cambridge: Belknap Press of Harvard University Press, 1963), p. 100.

12. See Harvey J. Graff, *The Literacy Myth* (New York: Academic Press, 1979), p.

19; David R. Olson, "From Utterance to Text: The Bias of Language in Speech and Writing," *Harvard Education Review* 47 (1977): 265–281. Cf. Jack Goody, "Introduction," in Goody, ed., *Literacy in Traditional Societies* (Cambridge: Cambridge University Press, 1968), p. 2; Brian Stock, *The Implications of Literacy: Written Language and Models of Interpretation in the Eleventh and Twelfth Centuries* (Princeton: Princeton University Press, 1983), p. 7.

13. Cf. David R. Olson, "The Cognitive Consequences of Literacy," *Canadian Psychology* 27 (1986): 109–21.

14. My pair of characteristics is a synthesis of Walter Ong's nine characteristics of an oral culture, Walter J. Ong, *Orality and Literacy: The Technologizing of the Word* (New York: Methuen, 1982), pp. 37–57. According to Ong, oral culture is:

1. *additive rather than subordinative*. This characteristic describes the tendency of oral cultures to structure discourse in a way that is convenient for the speaker, with long lists of items. The written culture, by contrast, concentrates upon the syntax, the "organization of the discourse itself."

2. *aggregative rather than analytic*. This characteristic describes the habit in oral cultures of using formulary expressions, such as pairs of words (an adjective linked with a noun or an epithet) as devices for aiding memory.

3. *redundant or "copious."* Here again, the characteristic is one that enables the speaker to present without a text, repetition helps the speaker recall and aids the audience in understanding.

4. *conservative or traditionalist*. Without texts to preserve important knowledge, oral societies devote considerably energy to "saying over and over again what has been learned arduously over the ages. This need establishes a highly traditionalist or conservative set of mind that with good reason inhibits intellectual experimentation."

5. *close to the human lifeworld*. Writing permits humans "to structure knowledge at a distance from lived experience [but] oral cultures must conceptualize and verbalize all their knowledge with more or less close reference to the human lifeworld."

6. *agonistically toned*. "Writing fosters abstractions that disengage knowledge from the arena where human beings struggle with one another. It separates the knower from the known. By keeping knowledge embedded in the human lifeworld, orality situates knowledge within a context of struggle." In addition, the oral culture is "highly polarized."

7. *empathetic and participatory rather than objectively distanced*. In an oral culture, "learning or knowing means achieving close, empathetic, communal identification with the known." Writing distances the knower from the known; there is no communal identity between the writer and the audience.

8. *homeostatic*. Oral societies live in the present, ignoring meanings or memories that no longer have relevance. Written cultures, by contrast, have dictionaries which record the "layers of meanings" that words have. In an oral culture the meaning of a word is controlled "by the real-life situations in which the word is used here and now. The oral mind is uninterested in definitions."

9. *situational rather than abstract*. "Oral cultures tend to use concepts in situational, operational frames of reference that are minimally abstract in the sense that they remain close to the living human lifeworld." Ong emphasizes that difference by noting that "an oral culture simply does not deal in such items as . . . abstract categorization, formally logical reasoning processes, definitions, or even comprehensive descriptions, . . . all of which derive not simply from thought itself but from text-formed thought."

15. This combines items 1, 2, and 3 from Ong's list. See Patricia Greenfield, "Oral

or Written Language: The Consequences for Cognitive Development in Africa, the United States and England," *Language and Speech* 15 (1972): 169–178.

16. This combines items four through nine from Ong's list.

17. See the argument by "Tribunus" that men can judge the first laws of nature even though not finely tutored. *North Carolina Gazette*, 24 March 1775, p. 1.

18. A poignant footnote is supplied by Andrew Bass, an Antifederalist delegate from Wayne County. Bass, who was blind, explained that "he could not understand [the Constitution], although he took great pains to find out its meaning." Elliot, *Debates*, 4:2.

19. For the population estimates and the census figures see Jensen, *Documentary History of the Ratification of the Constitution*, 1:300.

20. Charles Crittenden, *The Commerce of North Carolina, 1763–1789* (New Haven: Yale University Press, 1936), pp. 72–76.

21. Ibid., pp. 1–8; John S. Bassett, "The Influence of Coast Line and Rivers on North Carolina," *Annual Report of the American Historical Association for the Year 1908*, 1 (Washington: Government Printing Office, 1909): pp. 58–61.

22. See, e.g., Guion Johnson, *Ante-Bellum North Carolina: A Social History* (Chapel Hill: University of North Carolina Press, 1936), pp. 4–6.

23. James Madison, "Origins of the Constitutional Convention," in Gaillard Hunt, ed. *The Writings of James Madison*, 9 vols. (New York: G. P. Putnam's, 1901), 2:395. Madison alluded to that statement in the Convention, on August 28. See Adrienne Koch, ed., *Notes of Debates in the Federal Convention of 1787 Reported by James Madison* (Athens: Ohio University Press, 1966), pp. 543–44.

24. James G. Leyburn, *The Scotch-Irish: A Social History* (Chapel Hill: University of North Carolina Press, 1962), pp. 210–23; Duane Meyer, *The Highland Scots of North Carolina, 1732–1776* (Chapel Hill: University of North Carolina Press, 1961), pp. 69–101.

25. Donald Meinig, *The Shaping of America: Geographical Perspectives on 500 Years of History*, vol. 1, *Atlantic America, 1492–1800* (New Haven: Yale University Press, 1986), p. 347.

26. Ibid., pp. 190, 381.

27. In part the point is that merchants developed contacts outside their community, thereby increasing their national ties. Merchants also kept records, thereby impelling them toward literacy. See Crittenden, *Commerce of North Carolina*, p. 96. See also Crittenden, "Means of Communication in North Carolina, 1763–1789," *North Carolina Historical Review* 8 (1931):373–383.

28. Williamson to Martin, 19 March 1784, Governors' Letter Books, no. 5 part 2, NCSA.

29. Richard B. Davis, *Intellectual Life in the Colonial South, 1585–1763*, 3 vols. (Knoxville: University of Tennessee Press, 1978), 1:288–90; Edgar W. Knight, *Public School Education in North Carolina* (New York: Houghton, Mifflin, 1916), pp. 1–62.

30. Hugh T. Lefler and Albert R. Newsome, *The History of a Southern State: North Carolina*, 3rd ed. (Chapel Hill: University of North Carolina Press, 1973), p. 143.

31. Francois X. Martin, *The History of North Carolina from the Earliest Period*, 2 vols. (New Orleans: A. T. Penniman, 1829), 2:395. For an account of Martin's role, as a printer, in the transition from an oral to a written legal culture see Michael Chiorazzi, "Francois Xavier Martin: Printer, Lawyer, Jurist," *Law Library Journal* 80 (1988):63–97.

32. Elkanah Watson, *Men and Times of the Revolution*, ed. Winslow Watson (New York: Dana & Co., 1856), p. 253.

33. John Ferdinand Dalziel Smyth, *A Tour in the United States of America*, 2 vols. (New York: Arno Press, 1968), 1:161.

34. The estimate of a third comes from Charles Lee Raper, *The Church and Private Schools of North Carolina* (Greensboro, N. C.: J. J. Stone, 1898), p. 70.

35. Stephen B. Weeks, "Libraries and Literature in North Carolina in the Eighteenth Century," in *Annual Report of the American Historical Association for the Year 1895* (Washington: Government Printing Office, 1896):169.

36. Lawrence Cremin estimates the literacy rate at between 70% and 100% based on signatures on wills. See Cremin, *American Education: The Colonial Experience, 1607–1783* (New York: Harpers, 1970), pp. 543, 546–49.

37. Johnson, *Ante-bellum North Carolina*, p. 19.

38. Lefler and Newsome, *History of a Southern State*, p. 147.

39. Charles C. Crittenden, *North Carolina Newspapers Before 1790*, James Sprunt Historical Studies, vol. 20 (Chapel Hill: University of North Carolina Press, 1928), p. 11.

40. Ibid., pp. 24, 28.

41. Crittenden, *Commerce of North Carolina*, pp. 85–95; and "Means of Communication," p. 381.

42. Not until the state constitution was amended in 1835 did the sectional animosities subside. See Ora Blackmun, *Western North Carolina: Its Mountains and Its People to 1880* (Boone, N. C.: Applachian Consortium Press, 1977), pp. 130–133; Harold J. Counihan, "The North Carolina Constitutional Convention of 1835: A Study in Jacksonian Democracy," *North Carolina Historical Review* 46 (1969): 335–64.

43. Robert L. Ganyard, *The Emergence of North Carolina's Revolutionary State Government* (Raleigh: North Carolina Department of Archives and History, 1978), pp. 62–63.

44. Green, *Constitutional Development*, p. 71.

45. Ong, *Orality and Literacy*, p. 99; Havelock, *Preface to Plato*, p. 100.

46. North Carolina Constitution of 1776, Declaration of Rights sections 1–2.

47. North Carolina Constitution of 1776, Declaration of Rights section 21.

48. Havelock, *Preface to Plato*, p. 100.

49. North Carolina Constitution of 1776, Declaration of Rights section 4 (emphasis added). For a discussion of this provision see John V. Orth, " 'Forever Separate and Distinct': Separation of Powers in North Carolina," *North Carolina Law Review* 62 (1984): 1–28.

50. North Carolina Constitution of 1776, Declaration of Rights section 5 (emphasis added).

51. Havelock, *Preface to Plato*, pp. 93–94.

52. Enoch Sikes, *The Transition of North Carolina from Colony to Commonwealth*, Johns Hopkins University Series in Historical and Political Science, ser. 16, nos. 10–11 (Baltimore: Johns Hopkins University Press, 1898), pp. 69–70.

53. North Carolina Constitution of 1776, articles 31–32, 35.

54. Gordon S. Wood, *The Creation of the American Republic, 1776–1787*, (Chapel Hill: University of North Carolina Press, 1969), p. 158 n. 58.

55. North Carolina Constitution of 1776, article 44.

56. Jensen, *Documentary History of the Ratification*, 1:200–202.

57. Hugh Williamson to John Gray Blount, 19 March 1787, in Alice B. Keith, ed., *The John Gray Blount Papers* (Raleigh: North Carolina Department of Archives and History, 1952), p. 270.

58. Blount replaced Caswell himself, whose poor health prevented him from attending. Clark, *North Carolina State Records*, 20:129. Williamson replaced

Jones who declined to serve, writing the governor that he thought it would "not be in [his] power to attend there at the time appointed." Willie Jones to Caswell, 4 February 1787, Governors' Letter Books, vol. 7, p. 461, NCSA, reprinted in *North Carolina State Records*, 20:611.

59. William Pierce, a delegate from Georgia, described Blount in terms that suggest another reason for Blount's lack of participation at the Convention: "Mr. Blount is a character strongly marked for integrity and honor. He has been twice a Member of Congress, and in that office discharged his duty with ability and faithfulness. He is no Speaker, nor does he possess any of those talents that make Men shine;—he is plain, honest, and sincere." Max Farrand, ed., *Records of the Federal Convention of 1787*, 4 vols. (New Haven: Yale University Press, 1911), 3:95.

60. William Pierce wrote of him: "Mr. Martin was lately Governor of North Carolina, which office he filled with credit. He is a Man of sense, and undoubtedly is a good politician, but is not formed to shine in public debate, being no Speaker. Mr. Martin was once a Colonel in the American Army, but proved unfit for the field." Ibid., p. 96.

61. James Hutson, ed., *Supplement to Max Farrand's The Records of the Federal Convention of 1787* (New Haven: Yale University Press, 1987), p. 14.

62. Ibid., p. 144.

63. William H. Masterson, *William Blount* (Baton Rouge: Louisiana State University Press, 1954), pp. 126–27.

64. Koch, *Notes of Debates*, p. 154 (June 20) and p. 657 (September 17).

65. Keith, *Blount Papers*, 1:323.

66. Farrand, *Records of the Federal Convention*, 3:71.

67. Allan Nevins described Martin as the only one of the delegates who "opposed . . . the drafting of a new Constitution." Nevins, *American States Before and After the Revolution*, p. 406.

68. Williamson to Caswell, 20 August 1787, *North Carolina State Records*, 20:765–66.

69. Koch, *Notes of Debates*, p. 23 (May 25), p. 177 (June 23), p. 262 (July 10) (joint motion by General Pinckney and Martin), p. 378 (July 26).

70. Williamson to Iredell, 8 July 1787, in Farrand, *Records of the Federal Convention*, 3:55.

71. Of Davie, William Pierce wrote: "Mr. Davey [sic] is a Lawyer of some eminence in his State. He is said to have a good classical education, and is a gentleman of considerable literary talents. He was silent in the Convention, but his opinion was always respected." Farrand, *Records of the Federal Convention*, 3:95–96.

72. In spite of his lack of participation, Spaight somehow earned the modest respect of William Pierce: "Mr Spaight is a worthy Man, of some abilities, and fortune. Without possessing a Genius to render him brilliant, he is able to discharge any public trust that his Country may repose in him." Ibid., 3:95.

73. Hutson, *Farrand Supplement*, p. 175.

74. Farrand, *Records of the Federal Convention*, 3:74–75.

75. Koch, *Notes of Debates*, p. 237 (July 2).

76. For a biography of Davie see Blackwell P. Robinson, *William R. Davie* (Chapel Hill: University of North Carolina Press, 1957).

77. Blount to John Gray Blount, 19 July 1787, in Farrand, *Records of the Federal Convention*, 4:71.

78. Ibid., 4:95.

79. Koch, *Notes of Debates*, p. 260 (July 9), p. 480 (August 18), p. 509 (August 22), p. 534 (August 25), p. 569 (August 31).

80. Ibid., p. 656 (September 17).

81. Williamson to James Iredell, 22 September 1788, in Griffith McRee, *Life and Correspondence of James Iredell*, 2 vols. (New York: Peter Smith, 1949 [1857]), 2:241–242.

82. William Blount wrote to Governor Caswell on 19 July 1787 to report that the North Carolina delegates "were very unanimous." Keith, *Blount Papers*, 1:322.

83. Throughout the Convention, North Carolina most consistently allied with South Carolina and Georgia; though the state was also frequently in the bloc with Virginia and Pennsylvania. See S. Sidney Ulmer, "Sub-group Formation in the Constitutional Convention," *Midwest Journal of Political Science* 10 (1966): 294–96. Within those alliances, North Carolina began the Convention by voting with the nationalist group in favor of a stronger national government. See Calvin C. Jillson, "Constitution-Making: Alignment and Realignment in the Federal Convention of 1787," *American Political Science Review* 75 (1981):604–06. North Carolina, along with the other members of the bloc, was willing to have equal representation in the senate. But North Carolina was distinctively southern in insisting that there be a mechanism to change periodically the allocation of seats in the house.

84. See Masterson, *William Blount*, p. 135.

85. Farrand, *Records of the Federal Convention*, 3:83–84.

86. See Douglass Adair's essay "Fame and the Founding Fathers," reprinted in Trevor Colbourn, ed., *Fame and the Founding Fathers* (New York: Norton, 1974).

87. Farrand, *Records of the Federal Convention*, 3:83.

88. The conclusion to the letter stated that they had concentrated upon the "General pecuniary Considerations which are involved in this plan of Government." Although they did not mention more since they did not want to impose on the governor, it seems likely that those parts which they did mention were the ones perceived to be most important. Farrand, *Records of the Federal Convention*, 3:84.

89. Ibid., 3:83.

90. The reference is to United States Constitution art. I, s. 2, cl. 3.

91. Id. art. 2, s. 2, cl. 2. This provision was a response to the southern states' objection to a treaty with Spain giving up the right to navigate the Mississippi River. Debate on such a treaty had paralyzed the Congress throughout 1786 and into 1787. See Edmund Burnett, *The Continental Congress* (New York: Macmillan 1941), pp. 658–665.

92. Farrand, *Records of the Federal Convention*, 3:84

93. Ibid. The Fugitive Slave Clause is in art. 4, s. 2, cl. 3.

94. Farrand, *Records of the Federal Convention*, 3:84.

95. Farrand, *Records of the Federal Convention*, 3:84.

96. Koch, *Notes of Debates*, p. 27 (May 28).

97. Ibid., pp. 367–68 (July 25).

98. United States Constitution art. II, s. 1, cl. 3. The requirement is repeated in the Twelfth Amendment.

99. Koch, *Notes of Debates*, p. 573 (September 3). The language is included in art. I, s. 6, cl. 2.

100. Ibid., p. 599 (September 7). The language is in art. II, s. 2, cl. 3.

101. Professor Lynd views Blount's return to Congress as establishing that Blount was the courier between Congress and the Convention, helping to forge a compromise that banned slavery form the Northwest Territory while permitting it under the Constitution. Staughton Lynd, "The Compromise of 1787," *Political Science Quarterly* 81 (1966): 225–50; Professor McDonald sees Williamson as playing a key role in the bargaining between northern and southern interests. Forrest

McDonald, *E Pluribus Unum: The Formation of the American Republic*, *1776-1790* (Boston: Houghton, Mifflin, 1965), pp. 176-84.

102. Koch, *Notes of Debates*, p. 226 (June 30). He rephrased his suggestion a week later in language which suggests that he was not entirely sympathetic to the cause of the small states: "He seemed to think that wealth or property ought to be represented in the 2d branch; and numbers in the 1st branch." Ibid., p. 248 (July 6).

103. Ellsworth had said, "We [are] partly national; partly federal." Ibid., p. 218 (June 29).

104. Ibid., pp. 231-32 (July 2).

105. Ibid., p. 236 (July 2).

106. Ibid., p. 237 (July 2).

107. Ibid., p. 243 (July 5).

108. Ibid., p. 252 (July 6).

109. Ibid., p. 297 (July 16). In a rare indication of division within the delegates, Spaight noted his disagreement.

110. Ibid., p. 417 (August 9), pp. 453-54 (August 14).

111. Ibid., p. 453 (August 14).

112. Ibid., p. 278 (July 12). In the North Carolina ratification convention Davie explained his actions in this way: "It became our duty, on the other hand, to acquire as much weight as possible in the legislation of the Union; and, as the Northern States were more populous in whites, this only could be done by insisting that a certain proportion of our slaves should make a part of the computed population." Elliot, *Debates*, 4:31.

113. Koch, *Notes of Debates*, p. 269 (July 11). Earlier the same day Williamson had offered an amendment to the census provision to insure that blacks were counted in that process as well. Ibid., p. 267 (July 11).

114. Ibid., p. 531 (August 25).

115. Ibid., p. 506 (August 22).

116. Ibid., p. 190 (June 25).

117. Ibid., pp. 367-68 (July 25).

118. Ibid., p. 357 (July 24).

119. Walter F. Pratt, Jr. "Law and the Experience of Politics in Late Eighteenth-Century North Carolina: North Carolina Considers the Constitution," *Wake Forest Law Review* 22 (1987):577-605.

120. Ong, *Orality and Literacy*, p. 55.

121. Cf. Stock, *Implications of Literacy*, p. 18. "In societies functioning orally the advent of the written word can disrupt previous patterns of thought and action, often permanently. . . . One no longer responds through inherited principles handed down by word of mouth. The model is now exteriorized. Individual experience still counts, but its role is delimited; instead, loyalty and obedience are given to a more or less standardized set of rules which lie outside the sphere of influence of the person, the family, or the community."

122. Rhys Isaac makes a similar point in his "Books and the Social Authority of Learning," p. 246.

123. Newsome, "North Carolina's Ratification," pp. 289-90. The legislature ordered the printing of 1500 copies of the proposed constitution, for public distribution.

124. Newsome, "North Carolina's Ratification," p. 290.

125. Elliot, *Debates*, 4:3.

126. Ibid., 4:7.

127. The complete list of the principles was: "1st. A government is a compact

between the rulers and the people. 2d. Such a compact ought to be lawful in itself. 3d. It ought to be lawfully executed. 4th. Unalienable rights ought not to be given up, if not necessary. 5th. The compact ought to be mutual. And, 6th, It ought to be plain, obvious, and easily understood." Elliot, *Debates*, 4:9.

128. Ong, *Orality and Literacy*, p. 35.

129. Elliot, *Debates*, 4:8.

130. Ibid., 4:9.

131. Ibid., 4:10. Hermon Husband, the leader of the Regulators in North Carolina, made a similar complaint when he attacked lawyers for charging double fees. Those who paid the excessive fees, Husband argued, only made it possible for the lawyer to "study so much Sophistry and false Arguments and Glosses, that will blind Influence and confuse the Jury, as makes it necessary for the other honest Man to run to the same Expence." Husband, "An Impartial Relation of the First Rise and Cause of the Recent Differences in Public Affairs," reprinted in William K. Boyd, ed., *Some Eighteenth Century Tracts Concerning North Carolina* (Raleigh: Edwards & Broghton, 1927), p. 291.

132. Elliot, *Debates*, 4:11.

133. *North Carolina Gazette* (New Bern), March 24, 1775, p. 1 col. 1.

134. Elliot, *Debates*, 4:201.

135. Ibid., p. 189.

136. Ibid., p. 152. The use of the word "expressly" is an echo of Thomas Burke's (a North Carolinian) arguments to preserve the states under the Articles of Confederation. See, Burnett, *Continental Congress*, pp. 237–39. "Expressly" is intended to limit the scope or reading of a text to signal that the text retains its oral character as a report of what was said but not subject to elaboration.

137. Elliot, *Debates*, 4:44.

138. Ibid., 4:181.

139. Ibid., 2:62.

140. See Jack Goody and Ian Watt, "The Consequences of Literacy," *Comparative Studies in History and Society* 5 (1963):304–345, where the authors argue that "the intrinsic nature of oral communication has a considerable effect upon both the content and the transmission of the cultural repertoire. In the first place, it makes for a directness of relationship between symbol and referent. There can be no reference to 'dictionary definitions,' nor can words accumulate the successive layers of historically validated meanings which they acquire in a literate culture. Instead, the meaning of each word is ratified in a succession of concrete situations, accompanied by vocal inflections and physical gestures, all of which combine to particularize both its specific denotation and its accepted connotative usages."

141. Elliot, *Debates*, 4:93.

142. Stock, *Implications of Literacy*, p. 18.

143. United States Constitution, art. I, s. 3, cl. 6.

144. Elliot, *Debates*, 4:34, 36.

145. Ibid., 4:49.

146. Ibid., 4:71 (emphasis added).

147. Ibid., 4:150.

148. Cf. Michael T. Clancy, *From Memory to Written Record: England, 1066–1307* (Cambridge: Harvard University Press, 1979), chapter 9.

149. Elliot, *Debates*, 4:168.

150. Ibid., 4:201.

151. Ibid., 4:167. This concern is memorialized in the Ninth Amendment to the Constitution.

152. Ibid., 4:172.
153. "An Independent Citizen to the Honorable W. R. Davie, Esq.," 30 July 1787 (emphasis in original), in Boyd, ed., *Some Eighteenth Century Tracts Concerning North Carolina*, pp. 461–464.
154. Elliot, *Debates*, 4:144, 150, 165.
155. Ibid., 4:151.
156. The theme of opposition to a "consolidated" government permeated the Antifederalists' arguments. For two examples see ibid., 4:24 and 137.
157. Ibid., 4:88. See also ibid., p. 211 where McDowall contrasts North and South.
158. Ibid., 4:24.
159. Ibid., 4:104.
160. Ibid., 4:203.
161. Ibid., 4:157.
162. Ibid., 4:85.
163. Ibid., 4:57.

Notes to "THE GOOD OLD CAUSE": THE RATIFICATION OF THE
CONSTITUTION AND BILL OF RIGHTS IN SOUTH CAROLINA
*by James W. Ely, Jr.*

The author wishes to acknowledge the valuable research assistance of John B. Cutcher while a student at Vanderbilt University School of Law.
1. Charles Gregg Singer, *South Carolina in the Confederation* (Philadelphia: University of Pennsylvania Press, 1941), p. 18.
2. Lewis Cecil Gray, *History of Agriculture in the Southern United States to 1860*, 2 Vols. (Washington: Carnegie Institution, 1933), 2:595-596.
3. Forrest McDonald, *E Pluribus Unum: The Formation of the American Republic, 1776–1790*, 2nd ed. (Indianapolis: Bobbs-Merrill, 1979), pp. 171–181.
4. Allan Nevins, *The American States During and After the Revolution, 1775–1789* (New York: Macmillan, 1924).
5. For a discussion of the Pine Barren Act, see James W. Ely, Jr., "American Independence and the Law: A Study of Post-Revolutionary South Carolina Legislation," *Vanderbilt Law Review*, 26 (1973): 939–971.
6. An Act Authorizing Persons, Appointed by the United States, to Maintain Actions Within This State, March 17, 1785, in Thomas Cooper and David McCord, *The Statutes at Large of South Carolina*, 10 Vols. (Columbia: A. S. Johnston, 1836–1841), 4:667–668.
7. An Act for Investing the United States in Congress Assembled With a Power to Levy . . . Certain Duties Upon Goods, March 21, 1784, in Cooper, *Statutes at Large*, 4:594; An Act to Authorize the United States, in Congress Assembled, to Regulate the Trade of the United States With Foreign Nations, March 11, 1786, in Cooper, *Statutes at Large*, 4:720.
8. An Act for Appointing Deputies From the State of South Carolina, to a Convention of the United States of America, March 8, 1787, in Cooper, *Statutes at Large*, 5:4.
9. Ulrich B. Phillips, "The South Carolina Federalists," *American Historical Review* 14 (1909): 541–542.
10. Michael E. Stevens, ed., *Journals of the House of Representatives, 1787–1788*

(Columbia: University of South Carolina Press, 1981), 194. Henry Laurens was also named to the delegation, but he declined to serve because of ill health.

11. Some historians are skeptical about the contribution of several Palmetto State delegates. For example, Forrest McDonald characterized Charles Pinckney as "a brilliant and somewhat unstable young South Carolinian who had a penchant for political theory and a pathetic craving to be admired, a craving that he was willing to satisfy by outright deceit." McDonald, *Novus Ordo Seclorum: The Intellectual Origins of the Constitution* (Lawrence: University of Kansas Press, 1985), p. 209. McDonald described Pierce Butler as "an Irish-born nobleman who traced his ancestry all the way back to somebody-or-other but who, stripped of his genealogy, would scarcely have been noticed by his next door neighbor." McDonald, *E Pluribus Unum: The Formation of the American Republic, 1776–1790*, 2d ed. (Indianapolis: Bobbs-Merrill, 1979), pp. 268–269.

12. Ernest M. Lander, Jr., "South Carolinians at the Philadelphia Convention, 1787," *South Carolina Historical Magazine* 57 (1956): 134–135; A. S. Salley, Jr., *Delegates to the Continental Congress from South Carolina, 1774–1789* (Columbia: Printed for the Commission by the State Company, 1927). See also William Pierce, "Character Sketches of Delegates to the Federal Convention," in Max Farrand, ed., *The Records of the Federal Convention of 1787*, 3 Vols. (New Haven: Yale University Press, 1911), 3:96–97.

13. Malcolm Bell, Jr., *Major Butler's Legacy: Five Generations of a Slaveholding Family* (Athens: University of Georgia Press, 1987) pp. 19–81; James H. Hutson, "Pierce Butler's Records of the Federal Constitutional Convention," *Quarterly Journal of the Library of Congress* 37 (1980): 64–73.

14. George C. Rogers, Jr., "South Carolina Ratifies the Federal Constitution," *Proceedings of the South Carolina Historical Association 1961* (Columbia: South Carolina Historical Society, 1962): 48–49.

15. For a treatment of the back country see Rachel N. Klein, "Ordering the Backcountry: The South Carolina Regulation," *William and Mary Quarterly*, 3rd ser. 38 (1981): 661–680.

16. Frances Leigh Williams, *A Founding Family: The Pinckneys of South Carolina* (New York: Harcourt, Brace & Jovanovich, 1978), 221–223; Lander, "South Carolinians at the Philadelphia Convention," 135.

The extent to which Charles Pinckney made a contribution to framing the Constitution has been the subject of an intense debate. See Document, "Sketch of Pinckney's Plan for a Constitution, 1787," *American Historical Review*, 9 (July 1904): 735–747; S. Sidney Ulmer, "Charles Pinckney: Father of the Constitution?," *South Carolina Law Quarterly* (1958): 225–247.

17. Williams, *A Founding Family*, p. 271. For the political and economic views of Charles Pinckney see Mark D. Kaplanoff, "Charles Pinckney and the American Republican Tradition," in Michael O'Brien and David Moltke-Hansen, eds., *Intellectual Life in Antebellum Charleston* (Knoxville: University of Tennessee Press, 1986), 90–94.

18. Lander, "South Carolinians at the Philadelphia Convention," p. 155.

19. Farrand, *Records of the Federal Convention*, 2:389. Professor Lander termed Rutledge's motion "the most important addition attributable to the South Carolina delegation." Lander, "South Carolinians at the Philadelphia Convention," p. 153.

20. Farrand, *Records of the Federal Convention*, 1:162–163.

21. Ibid., 1:137.

22. Williams, *A Founding Family*, p. 254.

23. Ibid., p. 264.

24. Ibid.

25. Farrand, *Records of the Federal Convention*, 2:15.

26. Ibid., 1:124–125; Lander, "South Carolinians at the Philadelphia Convention," p. 152.

27. Farrand, *Records of the Federal Convention*, 2:449–453; Williams, *A Founding Family*, pp. 262–263. South Carolina's willingness to allow a simple majority of Congress to control commerce was part of a compromise under which Congress could not prohibit the importation of slaves until 1808. William M. Wiecek, *The Sources of Antislavery Constitutionalism in America, 1760–1848* (Ithaca: Cornell University Press, 1977), p. 73; Lander, "South Carolinians at the Philadelphia Convention," p. 147.

28. Wiecek, *Sources of Antislavery Constitutionalism*, p. 63. One scholar has emphasized the connection between South Carolina's determination to protect slavery and the state's role in the Constitution making process. Robert M. Weir, "South Carolina: Slavery and the Structure of the Union," Michael Allen Gillespie and Michael Lienesch, eds., *Ratifying the Constitution* (Lawrence, Kan: Univ. Press of Kansas, 1989), 201-234.

29. Farrand, *Records of the Federal Convention*, 2:371.

30. Ibid., 2:364.

31. Wiecek, *Sources of Antislavery Constitutionalism*, pp. 65–69.

32. Farrand, *Records of the Federal Convention*, 2:364.

33. Ibid., 2:371–372.

34. See generally Calvin Jillson and Thorton Anderson, "Realignments in the Convention of 1787: The Slave Trade Compromise," *Journal of Politics* 39 (1977): 712–729.

35. Farrand, *Records of the Federal Convention*, 2:453–454; James H. Hutson, "Pierce Butler's Records of the Federal Constitutional Convention," *Quarterly Journal of the Library of Congress*, 37 (1980): 68. For a discussion of Butler's role in framing the slavery provisions of the Constitution see Bell, *Major Butler's Legacy*, pp. 74–76.

36. Wiecek, *Sources of Antislavery Constitutionalism*, p. 79.

37. Williams, *A Founding Family*, pp. 267–269.

38. Farrand, *Records of the Federal Convention*, 2:632.

39. Williams, *A Founding Family*, p. 270.

40. For the documents transmitting the Constitution to Congress, see Farrand, *Records of the Federal Convention*, 2:665–667.

41. Charles Pinckney, *Observations on the Plan of Government Submitted to the Federal Convention* (New York: Francis Childs, 1787).

42. Charles Coatesworth Pinckney to Matthew Ridley, September 29, 1787, in James H. Hutson, ed., *Supplement to Max Farrand's The Records of the Federal Convention of 1787* (New Haven: Yale University Press, 1987), p. 278.

43. Charleston *City Gazette and Daily Advertiser*, December 15, 1787.

44. Ibid.

45. Stevens, *Journals of the House of Representatives*, p. 311.

46. Carl J. Vipperman, *The Rise of Rawlins Lowndes, 1721–1800* (Columbia: University of South Carolina Press, 1978), 241–252.

47. Jonathan Elliot, ed., *The Debates in the Several State Conventions on the Adoption of the Federal Constitution*, 5 vols. (Philadelphia: J. B. Lippincott, 1888), 4:316.

48. David Duncan Wallace, *The History of South Carolina*, 4 Vols. (New York: American Historical Society, 1934), 2:345.

49. Elliot, *Debates*, 4:316–317. In a move that has perplexed historians, Lowndes

voted to hold the convention in Charleston. This served to undercut the anti-federalist position which he espoused. Herbert J. Storing, ed., *The Complete Anti-Federalist*, 7 vols. (Chicago: University of Chicago Press, 1981), 5:148–149.

50. Stevens, *Journals of the House of Representatives*, p. 330.

51. Article XIII, South Carolina Constitution of 1778.

52. Willi Paul Adams, *The First American Constitutions: Republican Ideology and the Making of the State Constitutions in the Revolutionary Era* (Chapel Hill: University of North Carolina Press, 1980), pp. 207, 305–306.

53. Merrill Jensen, *The Documentary History of the First Federal Elections, 1788–1790*, 3 Vols. (Madison: University of Wisconsin Press, 1976), 1:147; Jackson Turner Main, *The Anti-Federalists: Critics of the Constitution, 1781–1788* (Chapel Hill: University of North Carolina Press, 1961), pp. 22–23.

54. Charles W. Roll, Jr., "We, Some of the People: Apportionment in the Thirteen State Conventions Ratifying the Constitution," *Journal of American History* 56 (1969): 21–40.

55. Charleston *City Gazette and Daily Advertiser*, April 29, 1788.

56. David Ramsay, *An Address to the Freemen of South Carolina on the Federal Constitution* (Charleston 1788), in Paul Leicester Ford, ed., *Pamphlets on the Constitution of the United States* (New York: DaCapo Press, 1968 [1888]), 371–380.

57. The *Columbian Herald*, May 8, 1788.

58. For an infrequent expression of anti-Federalist opinion see Charleston *City Gazette and Daily Advertiser*, Dec. 4, 1787.

59. C. C. Pinckney to George Washington, 24 May 1788, in *Documentary History of the Constitution of the United States of America, 1787–1870*, 5 Vols. (Washington: Department of State, 1905), 4:623–624.

60. Robert L. Brunhouse, ed., *David Ramsay, 1749–1815: Selections from His Writings* (Philadelphia: American Philosophical Society, 1965), p. 20.

61. A. S. Salley, Jr., indexer, *Journal of the Convention of South Carolina Which Ratified the Constitution of the United States* (Atlanta: Foote & Davis Co., 1928), p. 9.

62. Charleston *City Gazette and Daily Advertiser*, May 19, 1788.

63. David Ramsay, *An Address to the Freemen of South Carolina*, p. 379.

64. Elliot, *Debates*, 4:333–336.

65. Ibid., 4:306.

66. Ramsay, *Address to the Freemen of South Carolina*, pp. 379–380.

67. Elliot, *Debates*, 4:283–284.

68. Ramsay, *Address to the Freemen of South Carolina*, p. 373.

69. Elliot, *Debates*, 4:315.

70. Ibid., 4:337.

71. Jesse T. Carpenter, *The South as a Conscious Minority, 1789–1861* (New York: New York University Press, 1930), pp. 25–27.

72. Elliot, *Debates*, 4:272.

73. Ibid., 4:266.

74. Ibid., 4:337–338.

75. Ibid., 4:273.

76. Ramsay to Benjamin Rush, 21 April 1788, in Brunhouse, *David Ramsay*, p. 120.

77. Elliot, *Debates*, 4:313.

78. Ibid., 4:338.

79. Gordon S. Wood, *The Creation of the American Republic, 1776–1787* (Chapel Hill: University of North Carolina Press, 1969), pp. 366–367, 482–483.

80. Elliot, *Debates*, 4:314. Even some supporters of the Constitution argued that

the President should be ineligible for re-election. See the Essay by Cato, *State Gazette of South Carolina*, December 10, 1787, reprinted in Storing, ed., *Complete Anti-Federalist*, 5:141–144.

81. Article VI, Constitution of the United States.

82. Elliot, *Debates*, 4:265–266.

83. Ibid., 4:332.

84. Ibid., 4:290.

85. Ibid., 4:338. These comments prompted one correspondent to criticize "the inflammatory and menacing speech," and to dismiss the threats "as mere bugbears," *The Columbian Herald*, June 12, 1788.

86. Elliot, *Debates*, 4:283.

87. Ibid., 4:286.

88. Ibid.

89. Ibid.

90. Ibid., 4:259. David Ramsay also expressed the desire "that there might be added some declaration in favor of the liberty of the press & of trial by jury." He reasoned that "an explicit declaration on this subject might do good at least so far as to obviate objections." Ramsay to Benjamin Rush, November 10, 1787, in Brunhouse, *David Ramsay*, p. 116.

91. Elliot, *Debates*, 4:259–260. For the contention that a bill of rights was superfluous because the constitution created a limited government and all power not specifically granted was reserved to the people, see Essay No. 84 in Jacob Cook, ed., *The Federalist*, (Middletown: Wesleyan University Press, 1961) p. 575; McDonald, *Novus Ordo Seclorum*, 269; Wood, *The Creation of the American Republic*, pp. 536–543.

92. Elliot, *Debates*, 4:300, 315.

93. Ramsay likewise noted that the South Carolina Constitution of 1778 did not include a bill of rights. Ramsay to Benjamin Rush, April 21, 1788, in Brunhouse, *David Ramsay*, p. 120.

94. Elliot, *Debates*, 4:316.

95. Ibid., 4:316.

96. *Journal of the Convention*, pp. 13–23; Elliot, *Debates*, 4:338.

97. Charleston *City Gazette and Daily Advertiser*, May 32, 1788; *Journal of the Convention*, pp. 37–38.

98. Charleston *City Gazette and Daily Advertiser*, May 23, 1788.

99. Charleston *City Gazette and Daily Advertiser*, May 23, 1788; *Journal of the Convention*, p. 37.

100. *Journal of the Convention*, pp. 25–36.

101. *Journal of the Convention*, pp. 36–37.

102. *Journal of the Convention*, p. 38.

103. Elliot, *Debates*, 4:338–340.

104. Orin Grant Libby, *The Geographical Distribution of the Vote of the Thirteen States on the Federal Constitution, 1787–1788* (Madison: University of Wisconsin, 1894), pp. 42–44; Wallace, *History of South Carolina*, 2:343; Thomas H. Pope, *The History of Newberry County South Carolina, Volume One: 1749–1860* (Columbia: University of South Carolina Press, 1973), 55–56.

105. Charleston *City Gazette and Daily Advertiser*, May 28, 1788.

106. The *Columbian Herald*, 29 May 1788.

107. Charleston *City Gazette and Daily Advertiser*, June 19, July 15, 1788.

108. Ramsay to Benjamin Rush, 21 April 1788, in Brunhouse, *David Ramsay*, p. 120.

109. Edward Rutledge to John Jay, 20 June 1788, in Henry P. Johnston, ed., *The Correspondence and Public Papers of John Jay* 3 Vols. (New York: G. P. Putnam's, 1891), 3:339.

110. Aedanus Burke to John Lamb, 23 June 1788, John Lamb Papers, New York Historical Society, reprinted in George C. Rogers, Jr., "South Carolina Ratifies the Federal Constitution," *Proceedings of the South Carolina Historical Association 1961* (Columbia: South Carolina Historical Society, 1962), 41, pp. 59, 60.

111. Jackson Turner Main, *The Antifederalists: Critics of the Constitution, 1781–1788* (Chapel Hill: University of North Carolina Press, 1961), pp. 219, 249; Charles A. Beard, *An Economic Interpretation of the Constitution of the United States* (New York: Macmillan, 1913), pp. 248–249.

112. Roll, "We, Some of the People," pp. 30–31.

113. Rogers, "South Carolina Ratifies the Constitution," p. 59.

114. George C. Rogers, Jr., *The History of Georgetown County, South Carolina* (Columbia: University of South Carolina Press, 1970), p. 170.

115. Rogers, "South Carolina Ratifies the Constitution," p. 59.

116. Richard Walsh, *Charleston's Sons of Liberty: A Study of the Artisans, 1763–1789* (Columbia: University of South Carolina Press, 1959), p. 127.

117. Rogers, "South Carolina Ratifies the Constitution," p. 59.

118. George C. Rogers, Jr., *Charleston in the Age of the Pinckneys* (Norman: University of Oklahoma Press, 1969), p. 130.

119. Main, *The Antifederalists*, pp. 218–220.

120. Ramsay to Benjamin Rush, 21 April 1788, in Brunhouse, *David Ramsay*, p. 120.

121. Wallace, *History of South Carolina*, 2:343–351.

122. Ralph Izard to Thomas Jefferson, 3 April 1789, "Letters of Ralph Izard," *South Carolina Historical Magazine* 2 (1901): 203–204.

123. Pierce Butler to James Iredell, 11 August 1789, in Griffith J. McRee, *Life and Correspondence of James Iredell* 2 Vols. (New York: D. Appleton, 1857), 2:265.

124. *Annals of the Congress of the United States* (Washington, 1834), I (1st cong., 1st sess.), pp. 424, 705; George C. Rogers, Jr., *Evolution of a Federalist: William Loughton Smith of Charleston, 1758–1812* (Columbia: University of South Carolina Press, 1962), pp. 175–177.

125. *Annals of the Congress*, p. 753.

126. Merrill Jensen and Robert A. Becker, eds., *The Documentary History of the First Federal Elections*, 3 Vols. (Madison: University of Wisconsin Press, 1976), 1:148–149.

127. *Annals of the Congress*, p. 745.

128. *Annals of the Congress*, pp. 732–733, 739, 747. Smith opposed this motion, as well as other proposed amendments to change the form of government. Rogers, *Evolution of a Federalist*, pp. 175–177.

129. *Annals of the Congress*, p. 761.

130. Ibid., p. 773.

131. Ibid., p. 752.

132. Ibid., p. 913.

133. Stevens, *Journals of the House of Representatives, 1789-1790*, pp. 310–312.

134. Ibid., pp. 349–351.

135. Ibid., p. 351.

136. This was consistent with the rapid course of ratification in other states. Despite adoption by South Carolina, two of the proposed amendments failed to win the necessary number of ratifications. Robert A. Rutland, *The Birth of the Bill of*

*Rights, 1776–1791* (Chapel Hill: University of North Carolina Press, 1955), pp. 216–217.

137. Charleston *City Gazette and Daily Advertiser,* January 7, January 14, 1790.

Notes to CONSTITUTIONAL SILENCES: GEORGIA, THE CONSTITUTION, AND THE BILL OF RIGHTS—A HISTORICAL TEST OF ORIGINALISM
*by Peter Charles Hoffer*

1. The term "originalism" is the coinage of Paul Brest in "The Misconceived Quest for the Original Understanding," *Boston University Law Review* 60 (1980): 204–238. Alternatives are "intepretivism," "intentionalism," and "literalism." The reader will note that the references in this paper are a combination of legal and historical in style. That, if any excuse is possible, certainly fits the analytical structure of the paper.

2. See, for example, "A Bork Primer and Guide to the Confirmation Hearings," *The National Law Journal,* September 21, 1987, 31–38.

3. Robert Bork, "Neutral Principles and Some First Amendment Problems," *Indiana Law Journal* 47 (1971): 1–35; "The Impossibility of Finding Welfare Rights in the Constitution," *Washington University Law Quarterly* (1979): 695–701; but see a more moderate version in "The Constitution, Original Intent, and Economic Rights," *San Diego Law Review* 23 (1986): 823–832.

4. William Rehnquist, "The Notion of a Living Constitution," *Texas Law Review* 54 (1976): 693–706; Edward Meese, "Address to the American Bar Association," (1985); William Bradford Reynolds, "Power to the People," *The New York Times Magazine,* September 13, 1987, 116–122.

5. For example, Raoul Berger, *Government by Judiciary* (Cambridge: Harvard University Press, 1976); Lino Gralia, *Disaster by Decree* (Ithaca: Cornell University Press, 1977); Henry P. Monaghan, "Our Perfect Constitution," *New York University Law Review* 56 (1981): 353–396; Earl Maltz, "Some New Thoughts on an Old Problem—The Role of the Intent of the Framers in Constitution Theory," *Boston University Law Review* 63 (1983): 811–851.

6. See Larry G. Simon, "The Authority of the Framers of the Constitution: Can Originalist Interpretation Be Justified?," *Columbia Law Review* 73 (1985): 1482–1520.

7. See Hon. William J. Brennan, "The Constitution of the United States: Contemporary Ratification," Text and Teaching Symposium, Georgetown University, October 12, 1985. Other examples of the architecture of these arguments can be found in Laurence Tribe, *Constitutional Choices* (Cambridge: Harvard University Press, 1985) and John Hart Ely, *Democracy and Distrust* (Cambridge: Harvard University Press, 1980). A more philosophical approach to the problem is Ronald Dworkin's *Law's Empire* (Cambridge: Harvard University Press, 1986).

8. See, for example, the assumptions of both sides of the Bork controversy in Andrea Neal, "Robert Bork, An Advocate of Judicial Restraint," *ABA Journal* September 1, 1987, 82–86.

9. Though this question is one currently agitating historical scholars. See Lance Banning, "Jeffersonian Ideology Revisited" *William and Mary Quarterly* 3rd Ser. 43 (1986): 3–19 and Joyce Appleby, "Republicanism in Old and New Contexts" ibid., 20–34.

10. The reference is to Lochner v. New York, 198 U. S. 45 (1905) (in which the

Court voided a New York law limiting the hours of bakers as a "substantive due process" violation of the contracts clause).

11. See, for example, Ely, *Democracy and Distrust*, p. 73; Cass Susstein, "Lochner's Legacy," *Columbia Law Review* 87 (1987): 873–919. The role of the judge in modern public law litigation—suits involving classes of plaintiffs with institutions, agencies of government, or entire industries as defendants—invariably becomes more active than his role in private litigation. He becomes the ongoing manager of the suit and the remedy, rather than the passive umpire most lay people associate with judging. See Abram Chayes, "The Role of the Judge in Public Law Litigation," *Harvard Law Review* 89 (1976): 1281–1316.

12. James H. Hutson, "The Creation of the Constitution: The Integrity of the Documentary Record," *Texas Law Review* 65 (1986): 1–39.

13. The same point is made as a general caution by Mark Tushnet, "Following the Rules Laid down: A Critique of Interpretivism and Neutral Principles" *Harvard Law Review* 96 (1983): 781–827; and Paul Brest, "The Misconceived Quest."

14. An example of the difference between many law scholars and all working historians on this point. Many recent law review articles on the "republican" thought of the framers simply cite Gordon Wood's *The Creation of the American Republic, 1776–1787* (Chapel Hill: University of North Carolina Press, 1969) [e.g., Frank Michaelman, "The Supreme Court, 1985 Term, Forward: Traces of Self-Government," *Harvard Law Review* 100 (1986): 4–77.], though any historian familiar with the controversy over Gordon Wood's seminal work, for example, will concede that historians have not and do not appear likely to agree upon the ideology of the framers. See "Forum *The Creation of the American Republic, 1776–1787:* A Symposium of Views and Reviews" *William and Mary Quarterly* 3rd. ser., 44 (1987): 550–640.

15. "The American Constitutional Experiment," The Lynde and Harry Bradley Foundation Conference at the Kennedy School of Government, Harvard University, March 12–14, 1987. The exchange took place on the afternoon of the 13th.

16. Jack Rakove, "Mr. Meese, Meet Mr. Madison," *The Atlantic* 258 (December 1986): 77–86; H. Jefferson Powell, "The Original Understanding of Original Intent," *Harvard Law Review* 98 (1985): 885–948.

17. 2 U. S. (2 Dall.) 419 (1793).

18. *Georgia Gazette* (Augusta), February 10, 1787. The following account also relies on Kenneth Coleman, "Part 2: 1775–1820" in Coleman, et al., *A History of Georgia* (Athens: University of Georgia Press, 1977): 71–104; James D. Griffin, *Georgia and the United States Constitution* (Atlanta: Georgia Commission on the National Bicentennial Celebration, 1977), and E. M. Coulter, "Minutes of the Georgia Convention Ratifying the Federal Constitution" *Georgia Historical Quarterly*, 10 (1926): 223–237. Biographical Information was taken from William J. Northern, *Men of Mark in Georgia* (Atlanta: , 1907), vol 1.

19. The contributions of these men are recorded in Max Farrand, ed., *The Records of the Federal Convention of 1787* 3 vols. (New Haven Yale University Press, 1966), and James H. Hutson, ed., *Supplement to Max Farrand's Records of the Federal Convention of 1787*, (New Haven: Yale University Press, 1986).

20. Farrand, *Records of the Federal Convention*, 2: 665. Coleman, "Part 2," 95, speculates that Pierce and Houstoun would have signed as well, based on Pierce's letter to St. George Tucker, on September 28, 1787 (I . . . would have signed with all my heart had I been present.") Farrand, *Records of the Federal Convention*, 3: 100. As it happened, only Few sat in the Georgia Ratifying Convention which unanimously approved the document. *Georgia Gazette* Gazette, January 5, 1788.

21. On May 31, Pierce recorded in his own diary his opinion that the upper house of the federal legislature ought to represent the sovereignty of the states, while the lower house ought to more directly represent the people. Farrand, *Records of the Federal Convention*, 1:59. This should not be thought evidence that Pierce agreed with others, notably Pierce Butler of South Carolina, that the new Senate should represent property. On June 12th, shortly before he left the Convention, Pierce proposed to it that the salaries of federal legislators ought to be paid out of the public treasury (making it possible for a poorer man, like himself, to serve) and that the term of office for the senate should be three years instead of seven. Farrand, *Records of the Federal Convention*, 1:216, 218. Pierce was associated with the more democratic elements in Georgia politics, and sought to engraft that faction's values onto the new Constitution.

22. On June 29, in the debate over the New Jersey Plan for equal representation of the small states, Baldwin waffled on the nature of representation in the upper house. He wanted the upper house to represent property, and thereby give order to national politics. He was no devotee of democratic radicalism. Farrand, *Records of the Federal Convention*, 1:469–470. At the same time, he did agree to the "Great Compromise," although to regard him as one of its architects must remain speculation. Farrand, *Records of the Federal Convention*, 1:509, 516, 520. Coleman, "Part 2," pp. 94–95.

23. Pierce, "Character Sketches of Delegates to the Federal Convention" (no date) Farrand, *Records of the Federal Convention*, 3:87–97, reprinted from *American Historical Review* 3 (1897): 325–334. Pierce's diary, kept each day during his attendance at the convention, is far more revealing on his political views.

24. Followers of Clifford Geertz will find it a marvelous repository of cultural values. For the southern politician of this age (and perhaps our own), stature, physical attractiveness, and oratorical skills were measures of the inner qualities of a man.

25. *Georgia Gazette*, October 10, 1787; November 10, 1787.

26. *Georgia Gazette*, June 30, 1787; August 11, 1787.

27. *Georgia Gazette*, December 22, 1787. The introductory remarks were signed "A Constant Reader" but in the nature of such contributions were probably the work of the editor.

28. Coutler, "Minutes." The convention met for the first time on the 25th, but did not have a quorum until the 28th. The Constitution was ratified on the 31st, and the formal document transmitting the ratification to the Congress was signed on the 2nd.

29. *Georgia Gazette*, October 27, 1787; December 1, 1787, December 8, 1787.

30. *Georgia Gazette*, March 31, 1787. Periodic squibs continued the tale in later editions of the paper.

31. See, e.g., W. Stitt Robinson, *The Southern Colonial Frontier, 1607–1763* (Albuquerque: University of New Mexico Press, 1979), pp. 200–201. Georgia was not so involved in the last great war for empire, but her borders were still facing a foreign power, Spain, whose affection for the new nation, even in the best of times, was never great.

32. The argument in [Hamilton], *Federalist* No. 12 in Jacob Cooke, ed., *The Federalist*, (Middletown: Wesleyan University Press, 1961), pp. 73–79.

33. See William Wiecek, *The Guarantee Clause of the United States Constitution* (Ithaca: Cornell University Press, 1972), for a different view.

34. Farrand, *Records of the Federal Convention*, 2:64.

35. Albert B. Saye, *A Constitutional History of Georgia, 1732–1968* (Athens: University of Georgia Press, 1970), pp. 135–154.

36. Farrand, *Records of the Federal Convention*, 3:423.

37. In part the issue was an extension of the far more momentous dispute over the basis of representation. Rufus King, Gouverneur Morris, and others resisted the counting of slaves as persons, for purposes of representation, when domestic slave law regarded them as property. This animosity, dammed in the representation question by the "⅗ths" compromise, then burst its banks over the provision for ending the overseas slave trade.

38. Farrand, *Records of the Federal Convention*, 2:371–372.

39. Ibid., 2:371.

40. Ibid., 2:372. In fact Georgia did end its involvement in the foreign slave trade in 1798.

41. Betty Wood, *Slavery in Colonial Georgia, 1730–1775* (Athens: University of Georgia Press, 1984).

42. Tribe, *Constitutional Choices*, p. 30.

43. A slightly different use of the term appears in Ibid., pp. 41–44.

44. Guido Calabrasi, *A Common Law for the Age of Statutes* (Cambridge: Harvard University Press, 1982), pp. 172–177.

45. And standing itself is not merely a technical matter, but presents the central question of who is entitled to a remedy. See Joseph Vining, *Legal Identity* (New Haven: Yale University Press, 1978).

46. The issue of federalism, so hotly debated during the first term of Ronald Reagan's presidency under the rubric "new federalism," still divides historians. The latest edition of Alfred H. Kelly, Winfred A. Harbison, and Herman Belz, *The American Constitution* (6th ed., New York: Norton, 1983), p. 104, stresses the limitations upon federal government in the original document. These limitations, well understood by the framers, meant that the federal government did not have the clear right or duty to finally determine the meaning of the Constitution. Looking at the very same historical sources, Richard B. Morris has concluded that "The Convention prudently abstained from spelling out just what body would have the right to declare acts of Congress unconstitutional, but from the sense of the debates it was implied that the federal judiciary would exercise that power." *The Forging of the Union, 1781–1789* (New York: Harper and Row, 1986), p. 292. Constitutional controversies of any significance always have a historical controversy at their root.

47. A threshold question on the admissibility of the following evidence from *Chisholm*: are we arguing *post hoc ergo procter hoc*? I think not. The same cast of characters was involved in the resistance to federal jurisdiction in state debt cases in 1792, when Chisholm brought his suit against Georgia into the Supreme Court, as in 1787, when the state participated in and ratified the creation of the new government. To be sure, the debates in the new Congress over the funding and assumption plans, resting upon Hamilton's expansive views of federal power and his loose construction of the Constitution, were alarming to the Georgia delegation. Baldwin and the rest of the state's delegation joined in the Madisonian opposition to Hamilton's programs. Loose Federalist interpretation of the necessary and proper clause of Article I, section 8 undoubtedly heightened local fears of the federal judiciary, but the resistance of the Georgia congressmen to the Federalists in 1790–92 is an indication that *Chisholm* represents a consistent Georgia rejection of centralizing nationalism, not an aberrant reaction to a single issue.

48. The federal court system created by the Judiciary Act of 1789 consisted of very distinct courts of very limited jurisdiction, sitting in the states, circuit courts, sitting in the same districts, with broader powers, and staffed by one district court judge and a circuit-riding member of the five-man Supreme Court, and the high court itself. The circuit riding duties of the latter were not abolished until late in the nineteenth century (except briefly under the ill-fated Judiciary Act of 1801).

49. Judiciary Act of 1789, ch. 20 of 1 U. S. Stats. at 73.

50. Under a technicality: the section of the 1789 Process Act that described the actions available in the federal courts did not mention the writ of assumpsit, by which the contractee, having fulfilled his end of the bargain, sought to force the contractor to pay a fair price. Here the question was one of the so-called "common counts" of goods or services already delivered. It was a peculiarity of the writ-pleading or formulary system that still dominated private litigation, or "actions", that a debt could only be alleged if the exact amount was named in the original negotiations. Assumpsit evolved in English courts to give a contractee redress when the promise or work was performed, and the amount was not previously specified. Iredell was taking refuge in the technicality to avoid the larger question of federal jurisdiction over citizens of one state suing another, an issue he would have to face when the entire Supreme Court sat to hear the case.

51. 2 U. S. at 419–420.

52. U. S. Const. Article VI, sec. 2.

53. Embodied in the Judiciary Act of 1789 and the Process Act of 1789.

54. 2 U. S. at 453 (Wilson, J.).

55. Ibid., p. 419.

56. This particular question was raised at the initial hearing on *Chisholm* by Justice Iredell, for it had been the basis of his dismissal of the suit in the circuit court. Ibid. p. 429.

57. Ibid., p. 420.

58. Ibid., p. 422.

59. Ibid., p. 423.

60. The legal realists were a circle of law professors and jurists whose influence, in the early and middle twentieth century, profoundly reoriented scholarly views of the law. The Realists shifted the focus of writing and teaching in law schools from deductive formalism to empirical observation of how law actually worked in the society. See N. E. H. Hull, "Some Realism About the Llewellyn-Pound Exchange Over Realism, 1927–1931" *Wisconsin Law Review* 1987 (1987): 921–969.

61. 2 U. S. at 423.

62. Ibid. The notion of a state's sovereign immunity from suit has shrivelled with time. The federal and state governments have opened themselves to suit in a wide variety of areas, including tortious negligence, violation of civil rights, employment discrimination, dereliction of duty by officials, and disputes over welfare benefits. Much of this is governed by statute, but some is derived from the rulings of courts based upon readings of the federal Constitution (for example in equal protection cases).

63. Ibid., p. 426. On the remedial powers of courts, as understood in the late eighteenth century, see William Blackstone, *Commentaries on the Laws of England* 4 vols. (Oxford: Clarendon Press, 1759–65). The same notion actuated John Marshall's reasoning in Marbury v. Madison, 5 U. S. (1 Cranch) 137 (1803).

64. This mere collectivity theory of the state was also rehearsed at length by Wilson, infra. it was a very American theory, reflecting the visible coming together of the revolutionary movement, and its manifestation in voluntary associations and

committees. Compared to the organic model of Edmund Burke, or the Idealistic State of Friedrich Hegel, the collectivity theory may seem naive and unsophisticated. Nevertheless, it was based on the actual experience of nation-making, and expressed by two men who had a direct hand in that enterprise.

65. 2 U.S. at 428.

66. Ibid., p. 429.

67. John V. Orth, *The Judicial Power of the United States, The Eleventh Amendment in American History* (New York: Oxford University Press, 1987), p. 14.

68. See, for example. Justice Oliver Wendell Holmes, Jr.'s exquisitely tortured reasoning in Giles v. Harris, 189 U. S. 475 (1903) (holding that the Supreme Court did not have the power to remedy discrimination in voter registration).

69. This is my impression, though the characteristics of the judicial opinion of the eighteenth century may be an accident of the style in which these opinions were reported by contemporaries. Rarely was a reported opinion more than three or four pages long, even in the chancery courts, whose decrees often recounted the entire fact situation. My impression is reinforced by reading William E. Nelson, *The Americanization of the Common Law* (Cambridge: Harvard University Press, 1975).

70. 2 U.S. at 429.

71. Ibid., p. 430.

72. Ibid., p. 433.

73. Ibid.

74. Section 14, Judiciary Act of 1789.

75. 2 U.S. at 434.

76. Ibid., p. 445.

77. Altered in Santa Clara Co. v. Southern Pacific Railroad 118 U. S. 394 (1886), in which the Supreme Court stated, in a dicta, that a corporation was an individual, not a collective of individuals.

78. 2 U. S. at 447.

79. Ibid., p. 449.

80. Ibid.

81. Ibid.

82. Ibid., p. 452.

83. Ibid.

84. Ibid., p. 454.

85. Ibid.

86. Ibid., p. 455.

87. Ibid.

88. Ibid., p. 458.

89. Ibid., p. 464.

90. Ibid., p. 465.

91. The state assembly had proposed that local authorities might hang anyone trying to exact a levy from the public treasury pursuant to an order of a federal court—a clear threat to federal marshals acting to enforce a default judgment in *Chisholm*. Fortuately for the public peace, the Senate of the State did not concur. *Augusta Chronicle*, November 23, 1793.

92. 2 U. S. at 466.

93. Ibid., p. 467.

94. Ibid., p. 469.

95. Ibid., p. 472.

96. Jay was U. S. minister to Spain from 1779 to 1784, and well understood the

effects of our weak confederation upon his diplomatic negotiations. See Richard B. Morris, *Witness at the Creation, Hamilton, Madison, Jay and the Constitution* (New York: Holt, Rinehart & Winston, 1985), pp. 48–93.

97. See, for example, Charles F. Hobson, "The Recovery of British Debts in the Federal Circuit Court of Virginia, 1790–1797," *Virginia Magazine of History and Biography* 92 (1984): 176–200.

98. 2 U. S. at 478.

99. Orth, *Judicial Power*, pp. 19–20. The Supreme Court graciously accepted the verdict of Congress in Hollingsworth v. Virginia, 3 U. S. (3 Dall.) 378 (1798).

100. 3 U. S. (3 Dall.) 1 (1794).

101. Ibid., p. 4.

102. Ibid., p. 5.

103. Larson v. Domestic and Foreign Corp. 337 U. S. 682, 708 (1949) (Frankfurter, J. dissenting).

104. Amendments Proposed by the New Hampshire Convention, June 21, 1788, read into the record of the U. S. Congress July 21, 1789. Charlene Banks Bickford and Helen E. Veit, eds., *Documentary History of the First Federal Congress of the United States of America, IV: Legislative histories, Amendments to the Constitution Through Foreign Officers Bill* (Baltimore: Johns Hopkins University Press, 1987), 14.

105. Amendments Proposed by the Virginia Convention, June 27, 1788. Ibid., p. 19.

106. Amendments Proposed by the New York Convention, July 26, 1788. Ibid., p. 21.

107. Kenneth Coleman is convinced that after Virginia ratified, making the Bill of Rights part of the Constitution, Georgians decided that no action on their part was necessary, and so did nothing. Coleman letter to the author, November 19, 1987. The problem with this eminently sensible interpretation is that Georgians had already decided to wait two years (until Virginia ratified). Given the swiftness of their deliberations on the Constitution, Georgians' hesitancy on the Bill of Rights cannot be laid to mere inattentiveness.

108. Georgia Constitution of 1777; Georgia Constitution of 1789; William F. Swindler, comp., *Sources and Documents of United States Constitutions* (Dobbs Ferry: Oceana, 1972–1981), 2:433–466.

109. Bernard Schwartz, *The Great Rights of Mankind* (New York: Oxford University Press, 1977), pp. 81–82, suggests that Georgia modelled its text upon New Jersey's Constitution. This may be so, but another explanation lies in the stronger resemblance between South Carolina's first constitution and Georgia's constitutions. South Carolina politicians and merchants had far greater impact upon Georgia than did New Jersey's framers.

110. Linda Grant DePauw, ed., *Documentary History of the First Federal Congress of the United States, I: Senate Legislative Journal* (Baltimore: Johns Hopkins University Press, 1972), 168.

111. Robert Allen Rutland, *The Birth of the Bill of Rights, 1776–1791* (Chapel Hill: University of North Carolina Press, 1955), 217.

112. An historical summary is Orth, *The Judicial Power*, 30–151. Although the Amendment still has some bite, federal courts have exploited theories of implied state consent to expand their jurisdiction against state defendants.

# Contributors

**James W. Ely, Jr.**, is professor of law and history at Vanderbilt University. He is the author of numerous articles on the legal history of South Carolina and the editor of *The Legal Papers of Andrew Jackson.*

**Jack P. Greene** is Distinguished Professor of History at University of California, Irvine. He is the author of *Pursuits of Happiness: The Social Development of Early Modern British Colonies and the Formation of American Culture* and numerous books and articles in early American history.

**Peter Charles Hoffer** is professor of history at the University of Georgia. He is the author of numerous books and articles on American constitutional and legal history and *The Law's Conscience: Equitable Constitutionalism in America.*

**David Thomas Konig** is professor of history at Washington University, St. Louis. He is the author of the forthcoming book *The Constitution of a County Court: Law, Government, and Power in Colonial York County Virginia.*

**Edward C. Papenfuse, Jr.**, is Archivist and Commissioner of Land Patents of Maryland. He is the author of *In Pursuit of Profit: The Annapolis Merchants in the Era of the American Revolution* and numerous articles on the history of Maryland in the eighteenth century.

**Walter F. Pratt, Jr.**, is professor of law at Notre Dame University School of Law. He is the author of numerous articles on the constitutional history of North Carolina and a forthcoming book on the subject.

**Robert J. Haws** is chair of the department of history at the University of Mississippi and is a specialist in legal and constitutional history.

# Index

Abolition of slavery, 29–30, 40
Adams, John, 14, 15
American Revolution, 4, 13–14, 21–22
Annapolis Convention of September
    1786, 54
Anti-Federalists, 55, 56, 60–61,
    62–63, 64, 71–72, 75, 77, 78, 92,
    93, 94, 95, 96–98, 99, 108, 110, 111,
    113, 114–15, 116, 117, 118–19,
    121–22, 160 n18, 166 n156, 168 n49
Anti-slavery sentiment, 29, 30, 105.
    *See also* Slavery
Appleby, Joyce, 127
Articles of Confederation, 4, 18, 78,
    93, 102, 103, 105, 107, 111, 135–36,
    157 n2, 165 n136

Baldwin, Abraham, 7, 128, 132, 144,
    174 n22, 175 n47
Bass, Andrew, 160 n18
Bible, 4, 82
Bill of Rights, 3–4, 6, 7, 8, 34, 40, 42,
    43, 47–48, 52, 55, 60, 62, 63,
    64–67, 74–75, 96–97, 99, 104, 113,
    116, 120, 121, 127, 144, 152 n3, 166
    n151, 170 n91; ratification of, 7, 52,
    72–73, 77, 122, 144, 171 n136
Blair, James, 140, 143
Bland, Richard, 150 n15
Blount, William, 84–85, 86–88, 161
    n58, 162 n59, 163 n82, 163 n101
Bork, Robert, 125, 137, 138
Bowman, John, 117
Bradford, William, 143
Brennan, William, 126
Butler, Pierce, 27, 28, 102, 103, 106,
    110, 120, 167 n11, 168 n35, 174 n21

Burke, Aedanus, 117, 118, 119, 121, 122
Burke, Edmund, 176 n64
Burke, Thomas, 165 n136

Calabresi, Guido, 133
Caldwell, David, 93, 94, 96, 165 n127
Canada, 21
*Carlisle* [Pennsylvania] *Gazette,* 61–62
Carrington, Edward, 35
Carroll, Charles, 59, 69
Carroll, Daniel, 71
Caswell, Richard, 84, 85, 89, 91, 161
    n58, 163 n82
Charleston [South Carolina] *City
    Gazette,* 117
*Charleston* [South Carolina] *Morning
    Post & City Register,* 72–73
Chase, Jeremiah, 71
Chase, Samuel, 57, 62–63, 68, 69–70,
    71, 72, 73
Chastellux, Marquis de, 11
Chesapeake. *See* Upper South
Chisholm, Alexander, 134
*Chisholm v. Georgia,* 7, 125, 127,
    134–43, 145, 175 n47, 176 n50, 176
    n56, 177 n91
Civil War, 9
Coleman, Kenneth, 178 n107
Connecticut, 27, 29, 89, 132; and
    ratification of the Bill of Rights, 144
Congress, United States, 34, 120–21, 122
Confederation Congress, 33, 54–55,
    84, 86, 93, 102, 103, 107, 163 n91,
    163 n101
Constitution, United States, 35, 55,
    57, 70, 77, 78, 87–89, 93, 94, 95,
    105–08, 120, 127, 130, 131, 132–33,

134–36, 137–38, 139, 141–42, 153
  n9, 158 n11, 163 n88, 163 n101, 169
  n80, 175 n46, 175 n47, 176 n62;
  ratification of, 3–4, 5, 6, 7–8, 18, 20,
  21, 23–24, 28–29, 30, 42, 60, 65, 85,
  143, 144, 152 n3; importance of in
  South, 4, 5; and political parties,
  69; Supremacy Clause of, 134;
  Eleventh Amendment, 143, 144,
  145, 178 n112. *See also* Originalism
Constitutional Convention, United
  States, 3–4, 5, 6–7, 10, 18, 20, 22,
  24–25, 26, 27, 28, 29, 33, 34, 35,
  36, 59–60, 74, 77, 78, 80, 84, 85,
  86, 88–91, 93, 98, 102–04, 107, 115,
  127, 128, 129, 130, 131–32, 152 n3,
  163 n101, 173 n14, 174 n21, 174 n22,
  175 n46; Committee of Eleven (first
  Grand Committee), 85; Committee
  of Detail, 103, 104
Constitutions of individual states, 78,
  83, 158 n6. *See also* individual states,
  e.g., Georgia, South Carolina
Continental Congresses, 14, 17, 78
Coxe, Tench, 55, 72, 153 n9
Cremin, Lawrence, 161 n36
Cushing, William, 141

Dallas, Alexander, 134, 143
Davie, William R., 84, 85, 89, 90, 91,
  93–94, 95, 97, 99, 158 n10, 162 n71,
  164 n102, 164 n112
Dayton, Jonathan, 20
Delaware, 15, 16, 19, 20, 22, 25, 27; and
  ratification of the Constitution, 157 n5
Dickinson, John, 15
Dollard, Patrick, 113, 118
Drayton, William Henry, 18
Dumbauld, Edward, "State Precedents
  for the Bill of Rights," 65

Electorate, 57–58, 67, 69, 74. *See also*
  Representative government
Ellsworth, Oliver, 89, 132, 144, 164
  n103

Ely, James W., Jr., 5, 7, 179
Eubanks, Cecil L., 25

Farquhar, Robert, 134
Faw, Abraham, 61
Federalists and Federalism, 30, 41–42,
  55, 56, 61–62, 73, 74, 78, 92, 93,
  94–95, 96, 97–99, 102, 108–09, 110,
  111, 112–14, 115, 116, 118–19, 120,
  121, 128, 142, 175 n46, 175 n47
Few, William, 128, 131, 173 n20
First South, 10–13
Florida, 16
Forrest, Uriah, 56
Fothergill, Dr. John, *Considerations
  Relative to the North American
  Colonies*, 11, 12, 13
Fried, Charles, 127

Gaither, Elijah, 61
Galloway, Joseph, 15
Geertz, Clifford, 174 n24
George III, 141
Georgia, 5, 6, 7, 11, 16, 18, 19, 22, 23,
  24, 25, 26, 27, 28, 79, 89, 91, 106,
  113, 125, 127–45, 163 n83, 174 n31,
  177 n91; state constitution of, 7,
  130–31, 144, 178 n109; and
  ratification of the Constitution, 125,
  127, 128–29, 158 n5, 173 n20, 174
  n28, 175 n47; and ratification of the
  Bill of Rights, 127, 128, 144, 178
  n107. *See also Chisholm v. Georgia,
  Georgia v. Brailsford*
*Georgia Gazette*, 128, 174 n27
*Georgia v. Brailsford*, 140, 143
*Giles v. Harris*, 177 n68
Goudy, William, 95
Gough, Harry Dorsey, 72
Grayson, William, 29, 35
Green, Fletcher M., 82, 158 n6
Greene, Jack P., 5, 179
Grimke, John F., 111
Gunn, James, 144

Hall, Kermit L., 5
Hamilton, Alexander, 153 n9, 175 n47, Federalist #13, 15–16
Hammond, Rezin, 69
Hanson, Alexander Contee, 74
Havelock, Eric, 82, 83
Hawley, Joseph, 14
Hegel, Friedrich, 177 n64
Henderson, H. James, 17
Henry, Patrick, 23, 29, 36, 38, 40, 42, 44, 47
Hill, Whitmill, 99
Hoffer, Peter Charles, 7, 179
Hoffman, Ronald, 74
Hofstadter, Richard, 51
Hollingsworth v. Virginia, 178 n99
Holmes, Oliver Wendell, Jr., 177 n68
Homer, Iliad, 82, 83
Hooper, William, 157 n3
Houstoun, William, 128, 130, 173 n20
Husband, Hermon, 165 n131
Hutson, James, 127

Indian Wars, 129, 130
Ingersoll, Jared, 134, 143
Iredell, James, 20, 93–94, 134, 137–40, 141, 145, 176 n50, 176 n56
Isaac, Rhys, 164 n122
Izard, Ralph, 120

Jay, John, 21, 118, 141–43, 145, 177 n96
Jefferson, Thomas, 11, 34, 39, 42, 45, 51–52, 54–55, 56, 65, 120, 150 n15
Jillson, Calvin H., 25
Johnston, Samuel, 99, 157 n3
Jones, Willie, 84, 162 n58
Judiciary Act of 1789, 48, 134, 135, 138, 175 n48
Justice and the Judiciary, 6, 43–48, 97–98, 105, 133–44, 173 n11, 175 n46, 176 n62, 176 n63, 177 n68, 177 n69, 177 n77

Kentucky, 16, 26, 28, 30, 47
King, Rufus, 19, 175 n37
Konig, David Thomas, 6, 179

Lander, Ernest M., Jr., 103, 167 n19
Laurens, Henry, 167 n10
Legal Realists, 176 n60
Lee, Henry, 35, 41
Lee, Richard Henry, 35, 48, 66
Lenoir, William, 94
Lincoln, James, 113, 114
Local autonomy, 4–5, 6, 7
Lochner v. New York, 126, 172 n10
London, England, 13
Lower South, 16–17, 22, 24, 25, 27, 28, 29, 106
Lowndes, Rawlins, 23, 108, 113, 114, 168 n49
Lynd, Staughton, 89, 163 n101

McDonald, Forrest, 25, 89, 164 n101, 167 n11
McDowall, Joseph, 94, 96, 98
McHenry, James, 67, 70
McIntosh, Lachlan, 23
Maclaine, Archibald, 20
Madison, James, 18–19, 20, 23, 26, 34, 35, 39, 40, 41–42, 43, 46–48, 65, 66, 80, 84, 104, 120, 121, 153 n9, 160 n23, 175 n47; Federalist #10, 56–57
Magna Carta, 152 n3
Marbury v. Madison, 176 n63
Marshall, John, 37, 38, 137, 145, 150 n18, 176 n63
Martin, Alexander, 80, 84, 85, 162 n60, 162 n67, 162 n69
Martin, Francois, 81, 160 n31
Martin, Luther, 22, 27, 62–63
Maryland, 5, 6, 7, 11, 12, 15, 16, 17, 19–20, 22, 25, 27, 42, 52, 53, 55–56, 57, 60, 65, 110, 155 n28, 155 n30, 155 n31; state constitution of, 58–59, 67, 152 n3; and ratification of Constitution, 60–62, 63, 65, 66–67, 68, 70–72, 74, 152 n3, 155 n26, 158 n5; Declaration of Rights, 58, 59, 60, 62, 63–64, 66; state constitutional convention of, 59;

electorate of, 67–69, 73, 74, 155
n28, 155 n32; and ratification of Bill
of Rights, 72–73
*Maryland Gazette and Baltimore
Advertiser*, 53, 63
Mason, George, 19, 22, 23, 26,
34–35, 36–37, 38, 40, 43, 44, 58,
150 n15
Massachusetts, 19, 25, 27, 56, 65, 80,
130, 141; and ratification of the
Constitution, 60, 61; and ratification
of the Bill of Rights, 144. *See also*
Shays' Rebellion of 1786
Meese, Edwin, 125
Mercer, John Francis, 55–56, 69, 71,
73–74, 154 n10
Middle Atlantic states, 16, 22, 25, 26,
131
Monroe, James, 46
Morris, Gouverneur, 19, 22, 26, 175
n37
Mount Vernon Compact of April 1785,
54

Navigation, 88, 89, 105, 106
Nevins, Allan, 162 n67
New England, 11, 14, 15, 16, 19, 25,
30, 105, 106, 112, 131
New Hampshire, 21, 27, 28, 65; and
ratification of the Constitution, 144,
178 n104
New Jersey, 11, 15, 16, 19, 20, 22, 27,
30; state constitution of, 178 n109
New Jersey Plan, 174 n22
New South, 9
New West, 16, 17
New York, 11, 15, 16, 19, 21, 22, 25,
27, 28, 30, 65; and ratification of the
Constitution, 144
Nicholas, George, 41
Non-Originalism, 137
North Carolina, 7, 11, 12, 16, 17, 18,
19, 20, 23, 24, 25, 26, 27–28, 29,
77–99, 137, 156 n1, 163 n83, 163
n88; and ratification of the

Constitution, 77, 86, 139, 157 n3,
158 n10; state constitution of, 78, 82,
83–84, 91–94, 157 n2, 164 n123;
ratification of Bill of Rights, 77, 157
n3; Declaration of Rights, 82–83,
84, 93
Nova Scotia, 11, 16, 21

Ohio, 26
Old South, characteristics of, 9–10
Oral culture, 78–79, 82, 92–93, 94,
95, 96, 97, 99, 159 n14, 164 n121,
165 n140
Originalism, 125–26, 129, 133, 134,
135, 136, 137–38, 144–45, 172 n1

Paca, William, 62–63, 64, 66–67, 72,
152 n3
Papenfuse, Edward W., Jr., 6, 7, 179
Pendleton, Edmund, 41, 46, 51
Pendleton, Nathaniel, 128
Pennsylvania, 11, 15, 16, 19, 22, 25,
26, 27, 28, 80, 103, 130, 163 n83;
and ratification of the Constitution,
60, 61
*Pennsylvania Packet*, 63
Phillips, Josiah, 38
Pierce, William, 85, 128, 162 n59, 162
n60, 162 n71, 162 n72, 173 n20, 174
n21, 174 n23
Pinckney, Charles, 21, 22–23, 27, 102,
103, 104–05, 107, 108, 111, 112,
115–16, 122, 167 n11, 167 n16, 167
n17
Pinckney, Charles Coatesworth, 20,
27, 29, 102, 103, 104, 106, 107, 112,
115, 116, 162 n69
Pinckney, Thomas, 108, 110
Population, 28, 30
Potter, David M., 24, 30
Pufendorf, Samuel, *De Jure Naturae
et Gentium*, 39, 150 n15
Pratt, Walter F., Jr., 7, 179
Process Act of 1798, 176 n50

Ramsay, David, 28, 111, 114, 118, 119, 170 *n*90, 170 *n*93; *An Address to the Freemen of South Carolina on the Federal Constitution*, 110
Randolph, Edmund, 24, 26, 35–36, 38, 39–40, 43, 44, 103, 135–37, 138, 139, 143. *See also* Virginia Plan
Reconstruction, 9
Region, idea of, 3, 11–13, 14, 15, 16–21, 26
Regulator uprising of 1771, 82
Rehnquist, William, 125
Reid, Thomas, 140
Religious fundamentalism, 4
Representative government, 53–54
Revolutionary War, 101, 129, 141
Reynolds, William Bradford, 125
Ridgely, Charles, 64, 72
Rogers, George, 119
Rush, Benjamin, 14
Rutledge, John, 18, 22, 27, 28, 102, 103, 105, 106, 118, 167 *n*19

*Santa Clara Co.* v. *Southern Pacific Railroad*, 177 *n*77
Sectionalism, 31
Shays' Rebellion of 1786, 56, 130
Sherman, Roger, 29
Slavery, 4, 5, 6–7, 8, 10, 12, 13, 14, 16, 17, 18–19, 21–25, 28, 29–30, 39–40, 49, 87, 89, 90–91, 101, 104, 105–07, 113–14, 115, 116, 131–32, 150 *n*18, 153 *n*9, 163 *n*101, 164 *n*112, 164 *n*113, 168 *n*27, 168 *n*35, 175 *n*37, 175 *n*40
Smith, Samuel, 73
Smith, William L., 120, 171 *n*128
Smyth, John, 81
South Carolina, 5, 6–7, 11, 12, 16, 17, 18, 19, 20, 21, 22, 23, 24, 25, 26, 27, 28, 29, 42, 65, 80, 86, 89, 91, 101–23, 131–32, 134, 137, 142, 163 *n*83, 167 *n*15, 168 *n*27; and ratification of the Constitution, 102, 108–21, 122–23, 158 *n*5; Pine Barren Act, 102; state constitution of, 116,

120, 130, 170 *n*93, 178 *n*109; and ratification of the Bill of Rights, 122
Southern regionalism, 3–6, 8, 10–11, 14, 16, 17, 24, 26, 30–31, 34, 87–88, 91
Spaight, Richard Dobbs, 84, 85, 86–88, 89, 162 *n*72, 164 *n*109
Spain, 174 *n*31; treaty with, 163 *n*91
Stamp Act, 11
State's Rights, 5, 10, 45–46, 116–17
Stiverson, Gregory, 62
Stock, Brian, 95
Stone, Thomas, 57–58, 67
Sumter, Thomas, 116, 121, 122
Sydnor, Charles Sackett, 4

Tannen, Deborah, 158 *n*7
Taylor, Joseph, 98
Tennessee, 16, 26, 27, 30, 79
Tilghman, Tench, 72
Tilghman, William, 72, 153 *n*9, 156 *n*40
Treaty of Paris of 1783, 52, 142
Trenholme, Louise, 157 *n*3
Tribe, Lawrence, 126
"Tribunus," 160 *n*17
Tucker, St. George, 150 *n*18
Tucker, Thomas, 121, 122
Tweed, Alexander, 114

University of Georgia, 129
Upper South, 16–17, 22, 25, 29

Vermont, 16
Virginia, 5, 6, 8, 11, 12, 15, 16, 17, 18, 19–20, 22, 23, 24, 25, 26–27, 28, 29, 33–49, 79, 80, 86, 103, 106, 135, 140, 163 *n*83; and ratification of Constitution, 33, 34, 35–36, 40, 41, 42–46, 49, 63, 67, 77, 116, 144, 158 *n*5; "Declaration of Rights" [Bill of Rights], 36–38, 40–41, 58, 63–64, 66, 67; state constitution of, 45, 58, 130–31; and ratification of the Bill of Rights, 178 *n*107

*Virginia Independent Chronicle*, 40, 42
Virginia Plan, 130

Wallace, Caleb, 46–47
Walton, George, 128
Washington, George, 25, 26, 35, 40, 51, 52, 72, 157 *n*3
Watson, Elkanah, 81
West Indies, 12, 13, 101

Wiecek, William M., 105
Williamson, Hugh, 27, 80, 84, 85–91, 162 *n*58, 164 *n*101, 164 *n*113
Wilson, James, 26, 128, 140, 142, 143, 145, 176 *n*64
Wood, Betty, 132
Wood, Gordon S., 84
Written culture, 78, 79, 83, 92–93, 94, 95–96, 97, 99, 164 *n*121
Wythe, George, 41

The essays in this book comprise a complete discussion of the writing and ratification of the Constitution and the adoption of the Bill of Rights in five southern seaboard states. They reveal the interplay of a desire to protect states' rights, a concern for the preservation of individual liberty, and a defensive attitude toward slavery that governed southern attitudes. These concerns dominated constitutional discourse until the Civil War.

The South's peculiar "cultural constitutionalism" was first given definition in this period of American history, and as this book reveals, it initiated the process of setting the region apart from the rest of the United States. The events of these years were a necessary first step in establishing a southern regional identity.

**Robert J. Haws** is chair of the department of history at the University of Mississippi and is a specialist in legal and constitutional history.